Exploring Venice
Mindfully

Ruth Riby Howes

Dedication

This dedication is to Mum and Dad for taking me to Venice as a child and 'sparking' my lifelong interest in La Serenissima. As a family we didn't go on holiday to Spain because Dad refused to go to that country while General Franco was in power. While most people were discovering the Costa Del Sol and 'E Viva Espagna' we were instead discovering Italy and more particularly the family run Hotel Vianello in Lido Di Jesolo.

I have wonderful memories of glorious day trips via a crowded buses with 'standing room only' to Punta Sabbioni. The bus drivers calling 'Avanti Avanti' to get us to move further up the bus. Then onwards by ferry to Venice.

I really do remember that first sight of Venice from the ferry and the excitement of seeing the Doge's Palace & San Marco on the horizon.

Some years later the determination of my parents to find and visit the Venetian Archives was another special moment. With my brother Rob in charge of the map we set off into what were, in those days, the quiet calles across the Rialto Bridge in San Polo on a quest to find the Archives. Your enthusiasm for Venice & history was infectious.

In later years my family have discovered a small but incredibly special Pensione with a garden in Venezia. Short breaks have become almost addictive.

'Viva Venezia'

Acknowledgements

"Thankyou"

to my invaluable,
much loved,
highly individual,
'Home Support Crew'

To Nigel, Hetta & Mum, Dad

CONTENTS

Part 1

MINDFUL DAYS IN VENICE

"You fling the window open and the room is instantly flooded with this outer, pearl-laden haze, which is part damp oxygen, part coffee and prayers."

Joseph Brodsky

Mindful Venice

Whenever I visit Venice I notice something different and special. Each season of the year brings a different city. There is always a feeling of anticipation and excitement when returning.

Imagine ...

A city which closely resembles that of its Medieval past. Close your eyes and open them and you might be standing in the Medieval and Renaissance Republic of Venice.

The city structure has been unaffected by the impact of modern transport (and I include horse drawn carriages in this). The most significant impact was probably during the time of the Napoleonic occupation. Venice is timeless, its cityscape unaffected by the power of both cars and city planners. While most cities were developing their 'ring roads and fly overs' in the late 1960s and 1970s in an effort to totally transform city landscapes to meet the needs of the combustion engine Venice was instead coping with the damage of the 1966 flood and the start of the campaign to save the city from sinking back into the lagoon.

There are of course challenges for Venice linked to diesel engines and cruise liners. The plan to re-site the ferry and cruise terminal away from the historic centre is underway. Pollution from chemical refineries takes its toll on the buildings and the lagoon ecology.

However the basic template of the streets, canals and structure of Venice is predominantly the same as it was in the days when Titian and Goldoni walked through the calles and campos (streets and squares). The people of Venice have shown an ingenious engineering talent for finding solutions to the problems of their unique habitat. Venice is a modern city underneath the Gothic and Palladian façade. Modern extensions and new buildings do, for the most part, blend in or complement existing buildings.

Venice is the place for slow travel. Use this book *'Exploring Venice Mindfully'* to take time to explore the sights with greater depth and connect to the city. Plan your days with a different focus and in a different way. *'Exploring Venice Mindfully'* is structured in the same way as any guide book to enable you to explore the city. The difference is the addition of a layer of mindfulness as an overlay to your sight seeing. The mindful ideas and suggestions often have a multi-sensory focus and are designed to make memories stronger and last longer. Venetian inspired Mindful Moments are interspersed throughout the book. These are purposeful pauses for 'thinking differently' and they link to the sites of the city and lagoon.

There is a uniqueness to every day. Take it slowly. Break up the day differently. With a 'slow motion' approach make Venice (La Serenissima) the place to restore your own calm and serenity.

You may only have a day, a few days or a week to spend in Venice. However long you have to visit *'Exploring Venice'* will allow you to make your time in the city into a mindful experience – perhaps an adventure.

'Live in the Moment' in Venice & make mindful memories to take away with you.

"Venice, it's temples and palaces did seem like fabrics of enchantment piled to heaven."

Percy Bysshe Shelley

Essential Places & Spaces

First time travellers need to cover the essential sites of the city. There are certain essential sites which any first time traveller to Venice needs to visit. I certainly would never recommend focusing on mindfulness and missing the Rialto Bridge and market area.

The essential special places would include:

San Marco Basilica & Piazza
The Doges Palace & its Porticos
The Bridge of Sighs

The Rialto Bridge & Market
The Canale Grande
The Bacino and the Riva degli Schiavoni

The Friary Church (Frari)
The Salute Church

The Zattere
At least 2 of the campos
The Arsenale

The Island of San Giorgio
The Islands of the Lagoon
The Lido
The Island of San Michaele

Also visiting the six Sestieri (localities) to give a full flavour of the city. That's what's crucial when exploring Venice for the first time. To gain an impression of the whole city with many memories to take away when you leave.

There is a structure to '*Exploring Venice Mindfully*'
'*Exploring Venice*' is designed to combine strong strands of both sightseeing and mindfulness. You will find plenty of 'Guide Book'
information about the main sights. Alongside this there are regularly
interspersed suggestions for pausing and taking time out for a Mindful
Moment. These reflective and meditational moments are unique and
inspired by Venice.

The key sites are included along with some more 'off beat' places for
those who are staying longer in the city with more opportunity for in
depth exploration. Whether you have a day or a week you can use the
content of '*Exploring Venice*' to build days you will always remember.

Places to visit are grouped into times of day with a suggestion about
which time of day should be a good time to visit. Of course this is a
only a guide and it is perfectly fine to visit a campo in the late morning
as well as the late afternoon. However after much deliberation the sites
were organised into this framework of different times of the day. The
intention was that you could browse the different sections and choose
somewhere to visit in the morning, early afternoon and evening. In this
way you build an individual itinerary for a special day giving you
plenty of options for places to explore.

Alongside the specific sites are the ideas for creative mindfulness with
some longer *Multi-sensory Mindful Meditations*. As this is Venice
Italian phrases are used for these moments of mindful thinking or
'*pensiero multisensoriale*'.

Look out for these '*Momento di Mindfulness*' or '*Momento Meditativo
Multisensoriale*'. These are easily identifiable by this symbol. Think of
these mindful moments as 'page markers' on your journey through
Venice.

Practical Mindfulness

My view is that mindfulness needs to be part of everyday life. Practice is needed as we acquire the skills of living mindfully. We start by learning basic tools like the Body Scan Meditation or the Raisin Exercise and these are important. There are links to both of these in the reference section.

However to feel the full benefit there is a need to take mindfulness 'out on the road'. To use mindfulness in your working or home life. Mindfulness is also important at those times of the year when you have most time – when you are on vacation. Holidays should give us space and time to think, so what better time to put mindful practice into action.

'Mindfulness is paying attention to our present-moment experiences with openness, curiosity, and a willingness to be with what is, the capacity of our mind to not be lost in the past or future, but to be more present, to be less reactive.' This is the definition of Diana Winston from UCLA's Mindful Awareness Research Center. That phrase "the capacity of our mind to not be lost in the past or future, but to be more present, to be less reactive" is critically important. It's especially important when on vacation to avoid any 'pull back' to repetitive thinking about work issues or home tensions. Dwelling on those thoughts negates the positive effects of a holiday.

Mindfulness strengthens and deepens when we adapt a way of 'thinking differently'. With strengthened mindfulness skills we are more likely to focus on small things round us, noticing something we might have missed before. I'm acutely aware of the number of times I've walked to my car to go to work and missed a crocus or aconite flowering in the garden. When I take a mindful walk to the car I notice much more of the world about me.

With mindful thinking we notice thoughts settling and anxiety levels reducing. It's when we are on vacation and away from home and daily routines that we are more likely to give focused attention to the world around us and begin to notice things. What more wonderful opportunity than a holiday to focus on mindful thinking. There is an additional positive 'spin off' for general wellbeing. The mental and physical benefits of the holiday should be stronger and your holiday memories stay with you longer.

6

Mindful thinking gives us a different, what might be described as a more 'tuned in" way of processing incoming sensory information. This is the information we receive from the world around us through our senses. We then process and 'make sense of' this sensory information in our minds. In neurological terms there is something about mindfulness which means the 'firing and wiring' in our brains adapts and we start to respond differently. Many of the exercises and activities in '*Exploring Venice*' focus on enhancing multi-sensory thinking. The starting point is noticing how your senses respond.

So a mini break or a vacation is a perfect time to deepen your mindful approach to life. It's all about 'being present in the moment' and present and open to new experiences in a new place. If you can't switch them off then reducing the 'mental volume' of those troublesome thoughts about work. Mindfulness is about giving attention to each experience as it happens.

The approach in '*Exploring Venice*' gives special emphasis to engaging our senses and experiencing the world in more multi-sensory way. This might be compared to turning a 'black and white movie' into sharp digital 'technicolour'. If mindfulness is about becoming 'more open and receptive' then that needs to be the cornerstone of a mindful vacation.

Of course we may have to work on regulating our emotional reactions when we are travelling. As I write this I've just finished packing my suitcase for a trip to France and there is a worrying gale force wind outside and my 'travel nerves' are engaging. Regulating feelings such as escalating, unjustifiable anxiety (there really is 'no reason for it') is part of a mindful approach to life.

Diana Winston from UCLA points out that *"When your thoughts get caught up in fear or worry—'What if we can't find our hotel?'—you can recognize that it's just a thought and you don't have to take it so seriously. You can then come back to the present moment, where you're usually okay. Feel your feet on the ground and come into the present and you won't get carried away by thoughts that can sabotage a good experience."*

My partner and I did once forget the name of our hotel at Lake Garda. It really happened. We realised this towards the end of a long, five hour drive from Umbria in Central Italy to the Veneto. Thankfully we broadly knew the area where the hotel was located and found it without

7

too many problems. If mindfulness is effective at lowering stress levels, helping us focus and reduce emotional reactions when 'travel nerves' are engaging then it can only enhance a holiday.

My partner pointed out a few years ago that I had a tendency to 'crash' with low energy, almost approaching exhaustion when I stopped work for a week's holiday. For a couple of days I would be 'dragging myself around', just wanting to rest and sleep. This anecdote about tiredness is included because I've realised that I haven't felt this type of complete exhaustion since I began thinking more mindfully when approaching and going on holiday.

So we know that studies have shown that mindfulness is effective in reducing stress, improving focus and reducing emotional reactivity. All of which should contribute to a more relaxing and rewarding trip.

Mind Full, or Mindful?

Times of the Mindful Day:

Daybreak & First Light
Early Morning
Mid Morning
Late Morning
Mid-Day/Noon
Lunch- Early Afternoon
Mid Afternoon
Late Afternoon -Tea time
Sunset
Early Evening/Dusk
Darkness/Midnight Musings

And in Italian:

Alba
Mattina presto
Metà mattinata
Tarda mattinata
Mezzogiorno
Pomeriggio
Primo pomeriggio
Tardo pomeriggio -L'ora del tè
Tramonto
Prima serata/Crepuscolo
Oscurità/Riflessioni di mezzanotte

Timetabling – Planning an Itinerary
Each section of the day has a range of places to visit and things to do.
This enables the planning of an itinerary to fit individual interests and
the amount of time you have available.

Scenic Seasonal Serenity
Following the Mindful Day section you will find a further chapter
focusing on the Seasons of the Year. The music of Vivaldi's Four
Seasons gives the framework for this chapter.

The seasons in Italian would be *'stagioni dell'anno'* with:

Spring: primavera
Summer: estate
Autumn/Fall: autunno
Winter: inverno

The last chapter covers *'Farewell and Departure'* and coping with
returning home at the end of a holiday.

"We travel, initially, to lose ourselves; and we travel, next to find ourselves. We travel to open our hearts and eyes and learn more about the world than our newspapers will accommodate.

Pico Iyer

The Exploring Venice Mindfully Website
A website accompanies *'Exploring Venice Mindfully'*. This has a curated, evolving collection of photos. It was impossible to add these to the book. Some are 'mindful photos' taken on our trip to Venice when ideas for *'Exploring Venice'* were first forming. Photos and illustrations are included to give a stronger, visual dimension and add depth to the contents. The intention is for readers to browse and refer to the Website alongside the written text.

www.mindfulvenice.com

Remember to Pack Mindfulness

Don't forget to bring your home mindfulness practices with you on your travels. If you always do a morning Body Scan meditation then don't abandon it on holiday. If you have no prior knowledge of mindfulness then you should still be able to access the ideas and exercises and enjoy using this book as a guide to your exploration of Venice. What better time than a vacation to begin to develop new skills.

If you have a basic idea about mindfulness and some learning in the tools and techniques then you will inevitably be able to put the ideas in *'Exploring Venice'* into practice more swiftly. As all time away on vacation is precious it makes sense to spend a short time reading and preparing before setting off.

If you are relatively new to mindfulness then search online and browse through some of the information by John Kabat-Zinn. If you don't have enough time before travelling then certainly consider reading *'Wherever You Go, There You Are: Mindfulness meditation for everyday life'* on your return. Kabat-Zinn & colleagues development of MBSR (Mindfulness Based Stress Reduction) has been inspirational in the field of stress related wellbeing since the mid 1990s.

If you are travelling to Venice on a long haul flight then consider downloading some written and audio information for the journey. Some of the Apps for Mindfulness like Headspace or the more meditational focused bNirvana are a good place to start. There are an increasing range of these Apps with reviews and rankings. Browsing on UCLA's Mindful Awareness Research Center website would also give you essential background/downloads.

There are two particular tools and techniques which it would be helpful to know something about before starting your holiday. You don't need to study these in depth. You just need a basic awareness. The tools are:

> Raisin Exercise
> Body Scan

The Raisin Exercise is about being open to noticing details and differences and taking information from all our senses. All this achieved through slowly and consciously eating a raisin (or something else if you don't like raisins). There is a script in the Appendix. The Body Scan is a longer mindfulness meditation. Body Scan provides a structured transition into relaxation of mind and body. Tension is released, thoughts settle and you become relaxed.

Creative Mindfulness
Everyone finds their own preferences in style and content. I found Tara Brach's books and website were what finally got me consistently engaged in mindful meditation after several false starts. Later I discovered Camille Maurine and Lorin Roche's more practical multi-sensory, daily life approach. We're all unique and there is a wide range of mindful meditational approaches. There should always be a common core of *giving focused attention* and *living in the moment*. Some approaches are objective and secular while others are more spiritually based. Whatever your faith or philosophy of life you should be able to engage with the Mindful Moments without the need for any adaptation. In *'Exploring Venice'* evidence based approaches to mindful meditation are combined with a range of activities giving a more creative and imaginative dimension.

When writing about mindfulness previously I've always integrated it with positive psychology and appreciative and mindful leadership approaches. This is just not as relevant when writing about a holiday! Some positive therapy techniques have certainly found their way into *'Exploring Venice;* but the content is predominantly what might be described as 'Creative Mindfulness'. Basic mindfulness techniques with a more individual, creative overlay.

"In an age of speed, I began to think, nothing could be more invigorating than going slow. In an age of distraction, nothing can feel more luxurious than paying attention. And in an age of constant movement, nothing is more urgent than sitting still. "

Pico Iyer from The Art of Stillness: Adventures in Going Nowhere

Tools & Techniques

Slowing Down

Exploring a medieval city packed full of architectural and art treasures needs focused attention. Slowing down means you are more likely to notice details and enjoy the experience. 'Instead of a Race Slow down the Pace' is the phrase to remember.

Being more consciously connected, instead of automatic reactivity (aka 'running on autopilot') helps us make decisions and deal with daily difficulties. Taking a pause and breathing in a slow and steady rhythm helps to 'kick start' start this process of disengaging the autopilot. Moving more slowly and almost imagining you are in 'slow motion' is another effective way into this more conscious thinking. Be aware that often we think we have slowed down when we actually haven't really. Consciously thinking and moving in slow motion means we are much more likely to slow down.

Slow and steady breathing and movement has a more powerful effect than deep breathing. It's 'tranquilizing'! Slowing down the rate of thinking and movement is one of the tools you will find utilised in Mindful Moments throughout *'Exploring Venice'*.

Slow Travel

The Slow Travel movement is growing in Venice. Sustainable tourism is now a major priority for the city. Increasingly there are walking tours and boat trips which advertise that they have a 'slow travel' ethos. However at a basic level we can all bring an element of slow travel into our vacations. While visiting a place like Venice it 'just makes sense' to slow down and take in more of the details around you. Connect with the moment and allow for spontaneity rather than sticking to a pre-determined agenda.

Walking Mindfully

Walking mindfully must surely be slow travel in practical action.
Venice is the city for walking. When in Venice my partner and I walk
and walk … and then walk again. The Vietnamese Buddhist monk
Thich Nhat Hanh writes of 'walking meditation' and says:

*"To practice walking meditation is to practice living in mindfulness.
Mindfulness and enlightenment are one. Enlightenment leads to
mindfulness and mindfulness leads to enlightenment"*

'*Exploring Venice*' is all about planning your walks at different times
of the day so you maximise the sights you see in Venice and the Islands
of the Lagoon. This quote reinforces to me the reasons why I love
visiting Venice. The whole mini-break is a walking meditation, so it's
no wonder I return home feeling refreshed.

Tuning into the Seasons

Always try to be in tune with the seasons. In Venice there will be
marked differences depending on the time of year you visit. For
example, aspects of Venice like the mists in November, the Lido beach
in midsummer and the marron glace and panettone of Christmas.

It's important to consider seasonal characteristics like the weather, the
food and drink and even the type of scarves which people are wearing.
Remember to always go in search of seasonal serenity!

Noticing what's around you

When you are out walking look out for 'glimpses' of something
different, unexpected or special. It may be a sparrow feeding on crumbs
under a café table, it may be the view of the sunset on the horizon from
a vaporetto. It may be someone who simply nods, gives you a smile
and a kind word.

Some of the *Momento di Mindfulness* centre on noticing specific aspects of
the scenery of the city. Glimpses of gardens, courtyards, wells, stone
staircases, window boxes, campiellos, washing hung out, pink marble
paving on the floor of a palazzo, a chandelier sparkling in the darkness
of a winter's evening.

Go with the FLOW

It's important to occasionally abandon the plan and just go with the flow. The acronym 'Go with the **FLOW**' is useful and appears in the Mindful Moments.

Focus, **L**isten, **O**bserve & most importantly **W**ait before you say or do something. That brief pause before acting reduces reactivity. This is especially valuable when we are tired and irritable while travelling. Go with the FLOW is modern mindful thinking which fits neatly into daily life

Flowing breath

'Giving attention to the breath' is one of the most powerful ways of achieving relaxation. The inflow and outflow of the breath and the movement of the body when we breath helps tension flow away. By focusing on breathing we override the natural tendency to be on 'tense alert' all the time.

Remember you are at the seaside and you will be breathing in those negative ions charged by the sea.

Think of the Simple Things

What shall we do today? Snatch the 'here and now' and forget the 'there and then' (the exam results, the gas bill). Seize serenity. Just for today.

Appreciate the 'simplest of simple things' by noting down some things which made you feel happy or smile today.

Language Learning

When I'm trying to learn a language I need to focus much more than usual. I'm definitely in the 'here and now'. Spend some time learning a few Italian words for simple communicative scenarios like asking for a drink or a sandwich in a bar.

Learning to say 'thank you' to the cashier at the supermercato or reply to the Receptionist who greets you on your return to the hotel with 'Buona Sera' or 'Buongiorno'

Imagination and Metaphor

In *'Exploring Venice'* there are mindful moments which involve creative imagery or metaphor. Maybe it is imaging people in a painting out on the streets of Medieval Venice. Maybe it is compassion for the victims of plague. Adding this imaginative aspect is important because it gives depth and makes for a more creative mindfulness.

Emotional Reactivity has a Mindful Antidote

There is less in *'Exploring Venice'* about *self-compassion, loving-kindness* and *acceptance*. These aspects of mindfulness do appear in places but they don't have major roles. That's because the focus is on making a vacation a happy and memorable time.

The Mindful Moments are there to strengthen more conscious thinking patterns and reduce the effect of habitual and automatic responses. By changing these habitual responses we reduce reactivity. This should reduce upset and maybe even conflict with someone when we are in a 'tricky emotional situation.'

It's a necessity many of our brain's decisions and responses need to be automatic. This meant our ancestors stayed safe from that sabre toothed tiger lurking in the long grass. This is usually positive, in that brain processing space is available for more complicated decisions. We just need to swallow a mouthful of tea or blink without consciously thinking about it. It needs to just happen automatically. Sometimes though the autopilot goes in the wrong direction and into fight, flight or freeze response when it really isn't necessary. Over time this can become habitual and stress hormones are continually released and we are 'running on the tense fumes' and feel irritable and weary.

Taking back conscious control of our breathing gives us a strong 'way in' when we need to adapt and influence the autopilot - those automatic responses in our nervous system. Breathing is one of the few links between conscious and unconscious thinking. We can't influence our kidneys and adrenal glands directly. We can influence our lungs and breathing. Breathing is a bridge between automatic and conscious control.

This is especially useful because this includes control of learnt responses. For example when you see an email from Freda appear in your inbox and just noticing it means you are immediately pulled into a habitual pattern of anxious thoughts and reactions. Before you know it you have caught in a repetitive 'loop thinking'. This is about those times when your internal, incessant 'chatterbox of doom' is activated. 'Hello' negative spiral of thoughts.

On holiday an issue is less likely to be severe when compared to a difficult stress-filled scenario at work. But we can still fall into automatic reactivity on vacation if there is a problem with the plumbing at the hotel or a waiter looks momentarily unfriendly. I'm starting to think of this as 'irritable reactivity syndrome'. It happens when people start to become irritated by small things which they would previously not even have noticed.

The antidote is to decide if this issue really matters 'in the scheme of things'. It's unlikely it's at the level of risk of an approaching sabre toothed tiger. If it doesn't warrant an irritable response then just practice 'acceptance' and tell yourself that this is something minor and it is just 'as it is" and it isn't going to hook you in to reactivity. Over time this should become your new habitual response and then the autopilot can be switched on again.

Remember this is also true of the ruggedly determined voice of your internal critic (or internal bully). Segueing in and gently intervening with firm, positive words when your internal critic has got hold of your thoughts again.

Multi-sensory Mindfulness
When out and about exploring Venezia there will be a focus on encouraging you to make this a multi-sensory experience. Bringing on line all your senses when you are out for a walk. Listening for music, birdsong, breeze, voices and even sirens. Smelling the scent of the sea, coffee or fresh bread. Feeling that slight coolness as an incoming breath moves through your nose. Noticing the warmth of the sun or the touch of a smooth cold marble surface. Focusing on the horizon and the changes of light and how colours change during the day. Noticing the flavour of herbs and spices and savouring the taste while you eat.

Drawing on all your senses. More than anything else a multi-sensory approach gives us a template for developing a whole life approach to mindfulness.

Meditation range - Scents from the East

Pack at least one bottle of essential oil. It will enhance mindful moments and simply make where you are staying a pleasanter place. If you only have one oil with you then use it throughout your vacation. Sprinkle it on the bed. Fill the sink with hot water, add a few drops and let the scent diffuse throughout the room. After the holiday you will associate the scent with a happy time.

Choose oils with a connection to meditation such as Lavender, Bergamot, Nutmeg, Cedarwood, Benzoin, Frankincense, Ylang Ylang, Orange, Patchouli, Rose Geranium and Clary Sage.

Make your own blend of oils and add to water to make an air freshener, a reviving spray or to sprinkle on strange beds. Inhaling the scent from a handkerchief is a very easy way to access oils when travelling. Choose an aromatic hand cream and foot balm or make one with your own blend.

Cedar oil is one suggestion because it is a more unusual oil. It's woody, long lasting and meditational. It is readily available because it's used to deter moths. This means it can be located in shops for a very low price. Cedar oil is a strong scent. On a balmy summer's day you can almost smell the oil in the air. Evergreen trees have this wonderful resin scent. Cedar is one of the trees which grows in Venice and out in the wilder reaches of the lagoon. Look out for cedar trees in the Giardini Gardens.

Time to Visit Definitions

Mindfulness is consciously "paying attention on purpose, in the present moment, and non-judgmentally." (John Kabat-Zinn). I like to think of it as 'giving attention' rather than 'paying attention' as it makes the action a more conscious decision. Mindfulness is also about 'being kind' in the way you think about and treat people, including how you treat yourself. We are often our own most harsh critic. Kristin Neff suggests the incredibly useful strategy of purposefully interrupting that critical inner voice, pausing and imagining what a good friend might say to you in this same situation. The friend's voice would probably be more gentle and kind, even when you have done something which you regret. Melanie Greenberg in The Stress-Proof Brain calls mindfulness "an open, compassionate attitude toward your inner experience."

Lorin Roche adds that "one of the definitions of meditation is to be there at the gates of perception, noticing what comes and goes. In breathing meditation, notice the air as it flows in, turns, and flows out, then turns to flow in. Be there and feel the contact, you and the vast ocean of air."

Mindfulness meditation is a time to stay present with thoughts, feelings and bodily sensations without making critical judgements and reducing levels of emotional reactivity. Mindful Meditation should boost energy levels, turn down the volume of stress and revive the spirits.

Continue making Connections

In practical terms mindfulness is about connecting with both your internal state (thoughts and bodily sensations) and the environment around you. By following the ideas in '*Exploring Venice*' you will experience more of the city as well as strengthening your mindfulness. In simple terms it's about using a few simple strategies:

- Continue *giving attention* and *noticing* the people and things around you
- Pause and integrate *mindful moments* into each day and begin to *think mindfully*
- *self monitor* your *emotional reactivity* and treat yourself *kindly*
- Continue *daily practice* - keep that capsule of contained practice
- *Mindfully Meander* – don't always stick to the plan (and that's the case whether you're on holiday or at home).

Utilising these strategies means you should get more out of your holiday. The rest of the book is about how to put this into action while 'out and about' in Venice.

Pack your Mindfulness Kit

Consider packing:

An audio or script for Body Scan mindful meditation
A Journal or notebook
A small sized diffuser (for essential oils)
An essential oil (or oils)
Candle or tea-light
A small water spray or empty spray bottle
Aromatic foot balm and hand cream
Blister plasters … there is a lot of walking

If you forget to pack then don't worry. You can stream a Body Scan mediation. You can buy a journal and foot cream. You can use the sink to diffuse essential oils.

Tuning out by Tuning in.....
Sometimes when we go on vacation we need a mental transition period where we overcome that feeling of continual 'busy-ness' and any residual mental weariness. Instead of continuing to press firmly on the accelerator we need to 'take our foot off the accelerator of speedy living' and just glide along. Transition to 'holiday mode' and begin to feel revived.

It's time to linger a little longer. Time to change habitual patterns of thinking and behaviour. What better time to live mindfully for a few days.

Mindful travel is about relaxed attentiveness. The changes may be tiny, barely noticeable changes in daily life. Notice those changes in how you react and respond to events during each day.

Focused Attention – what is attention?
Attention and more specifically *joint attention* is the most fundamental developmental skill. Without developing shared attention with others which means engaging in joint looking and listening, a child struggles to learn. It is that basic.

There are several stages of development of 'attention control'. These were first identified by Reynell (1976). An infant begins life with fleeting sporadic attention. Their attention flits from one stimuli to another with rapid changes in focus. Then over time and through interactions with adults this fleeting focus moves to more single channelled attention. This is the stage where only one stimuli is focused on at a time. A child becomes engrossed and pays total attention to one activity.

The next stage is when the child becomes able to respond to some interruptions (bids for their attention) and to respond to an adult and pay attention to what that adult is communicating to them. The skill develops till eventually the child can choose to stop and listen without specific reminders. The child still needs to stop what they are doing and look at the person speaking to them. This ability to deal with an interruption and then move back to the previous task (without forgetting what they were doing) strengthens.

Eventually the child develops integrated attention where it is possible to both listen and carry out a task at the same time. Only at this point can a child really learn and participate successfully in a group.

Reynell pointed out that at times of stress, attention can break down to an earlier developmental level. I've realised while working on mindfulness in practical daily life settings that this 'breakdown' is the case for adults as well as children. When I'm stressed I can't focus and my attention flits randomly from thought to thought. I find it hard to settle on a job or listen to what someone is saying to me.

I've worked professionally with the development of attention and helping children build those crucial skills of joint attention in communication with others throughout my career as a specialist therapist. I was wavering whether to edit this out but decided to retain it as it gives greater insight into how 'attention' functions in life.

We all talk about 'attention' and paying attention, including in relation to mindfulness, but most of us know little about it as a distinct skill. As with any skill some are better at it than others, some are naturally gifted and others have to work hard at it. My apologies for those keen to get on to sight-seeing for this intentional attentional de-tour!

Creating a Mindful Journal

Throughout history people have kept travel journals. We have insight into the ancient Roman world and the events surrounding the eruption of Vesuvius which devastated Pompeii and Herculaneum because of the journals of Pliny.

Writing about our emotions and thoughts helps us experience a greater sense of wellbeing. This is the case for both emotional and physical health. Studies show that writing about our emotions can actually mean fewer visits to the doctor and reduced sickness from work. Journaling seems to support a stronger immune system. Of course usually our writing would be about stressors in life such as relationships or 'troubling' events at work. Reflective writing helps us to process experience and find meaning and patterns about the causes of stress. What's happened and how to move on. Pennebaker has led much of the research on the positive effects of expressive writing through journaling (2016).

What's odd is that few of us actually have the stamina to write, even for just the four days, which one study suggested was all that was needed to help people feel calmer and stronger.

Writing down our thoughts has a powerfully positive effect in reducing stress and supporting positivity. Writing about whatever is making us feel anxious seems to reduce the level of anxiety. What's not to like?

Keeping a journal on any vacation is part of a mindful approach. A Mindful Log is all about appreciating your journey. Noting your impressions, insights and special moments. Because research says that a journal facilitates positive thinking, even when only a few minutes a day is spent writing, then logic suggests that journaling must 'extra enhance' a holiday experience and create a strong store of memories.

It's re-assuring to know that writing a string of single words in a journal entry can be just as positive as writing a page. These 'single word journals' act as reminders of thoughts and ideas we experienced that day. Syntax (grammar) is abandoned! Anything goes! Sketches, drawings or mind maps make great journal entries. I've decided I'm going to try using mind maps as a log of each day on my next mini-break.

So if you don't find writing a pleasure then just jot down a string of single words. Maybe arrange the words in a pattern on the page.

Throughout '*Exploring Venice*' there is a theme of making memories stronger through photos, soundtracks or journaling. It's all about capturing the experiences of the day.

For the more technically minded there are online diaries. 'Five minutes' is an online diary with its roots in positive psychology and is geared to short reflective entries. There are many online journals such as Penzu and Evernotes available. I use Evernotes when researching writing a book as it helps me structure and organise my ideas more effectively than in a word document. These days there is something out there to suit everyone.

There are other simple diaries ranging from some sheets of paper folded and clipped together to a specially chosen, beautifully illustrated journal. Of course the next step is to decide which pen to choose to write with ... If you prefer a handwritten journal then watch out for the Venetian stationery shops. If you look carefully you should find an inexpensive notebook to make into your holiday journal.

Find somewhere to sit with a journal (or even just a piece of paper) and jot down thoughts, feelings and experiences. Maybe reflect on the day's events taking a multi-sensory approach. Remember anything you've seen, heard or tasted is 'noteworthy'.

Occasionally I might sit on a bench or in a café and make written observations in 'real time'. Mostly that's while watching the garden or river. Real time journaling helps me focus and notice what's happening in the world around me.

Experiment and find an approach which works for you. Then take it home and use it to cope with any 'troublesome issues' in your life when the holiday ends.

Mindfulness Apps
Mindfulness Apps like Calm, Headspace or Insight Timer can be effective when you want to focus on a structured meditation simply to help you cope with a long journey. The Apps give structured meditations and soundtracks and help you to serenely step out from the stress of chaotic travel. Most have free basic versions. Five minutes to re-boot our positive thinking.

Templates for Long and Short Mindful Meditations

Sensory Travel
'*Exploring Venice*' uses a multi-sensory approach in order to add depth to holiday experiences and create memories which are more enduring. You will be exploring the sites with this slightly different multi-sensory perspective.

'Sensory travel' involves focusing on the world around us when we travel rather than getting stuck in pre-occupations about practicalities.

"I've remembered the lesson about the senses and, when I go someplace new, I try to notice what my senses are picking up on, what I'm feeling, and what's going on around me. It has made travel much more memorable and enjoyable." Matt Hershberger (2017)

The message is to focus on your senses and notice what each sense is picking up on and what's happening around you.

Energy Boosting Meditation (a short meditation)
This is a template for a short mindful meditation. There are many others and this is provided as an example and basic guide in case you need that.

Focus on your breathing. Take a breath. Make a conscious effort to breathe slowly and steadily.

Imagine your whole body breathing in and breathing out.

Bring in background sensations and what's on your mind, any emotional responses and thoughts.

Be aware of the vastness of space and time around you.

Welcome any thoughts which arrive in your mind, even those connected with any To Do list you left at home. Visiting thoughts are not something to care much about.

Just notice any background noise- it's not a problem.

Melt into rest. Soften your body. Be aware of bodily sensations and how they change.

Get into a Rhythm - speed up and slow down your thoughts.

Return to your breathing – continue to breathe slowly and steadily.

By reaching this calm place you are rested. Renewing flagging energy levels

Strengthening with mindfulness, ready to go out and give attention to exploring the sights of the city.

'Re-boot' Thinking

Lorin Roche has a unique and creative approach to bringing meditation into everyday life. This multi- sensory approach gives a way to strengthen skills in focused attention. It's also a way of re-booting thinking to a more mindful mode when we're feeling tired or distracted.

If you are able, then take time for a longer meditation (more than 10 minutes) each day. This can be a basic Body Scan or a guided auditory meditation. What follows is a template for a longer multi-sensory mindful meditation. Each time you take time out and go through the meditation sequence you are learning more about yourself and your sensory preferences.

Strengthening Sensory Attention (a longer meditation)

In effect what follows is a sequence of mini meditations. Each of the senses is visited in turn and they become connected. Over time, the more you practice, the more you will begin to tune in and notice how your senses react and function outside of the meditation when you are out and about in daily life.

You will need a drink, an essential oil, something to hold which has a soft or interesting texture (a handkerchief or a silk scarf, a stone.)

26

Starting Point

Sit quietly. Take slow and steady breaths as you transition into a mindful mediational place.

Taste - Take a sip of water or tea and move through the sensations in mouth and throat as you swallow.

Movement - focus on your hands next. Move your fingers slowly and feel the feedback as they move through the air and note any sensations. Move in very slow motion. Clench and unclench your hands. Clench and unclench your toes.

Smell - the essential oil in the burner. When you do this meditation again you can prepare by choosing an item with a scent and holding it and breathing in the scent.

Listening - listen to any sounds around you and how far away they are.

Sight - gaze around and notice a specific colour and focus on it. Close your eyes and still see the colour in your mind. Open your eyes and widen your gaze to the corners of the room and the ceiling....up, down and all around. Notice the outline of the shapes around you.

Touch & Texture - with preparation you can have something ready to actually hold and contemplate. Imagine feeling a soft comfortable sheet or blanket around you.

Space - the sensation of space is special. With closed eyes gently wriggle your fingers and then let your arms drop to your sides and move your arms slowly backwards and forwards through space.

Balance - feel centred and poised. Gradually move your head back a little. Make small gentle movements of neck in gentle head rolling in a circular pattern.

Sensory Sight Seeing

You are enriching the way you think and enhancing your sensory thinking. The pictures in your mind will become richer and more textured with visual and auditory aspects. By adding more layers to the experience your holiday memories should be more vivid and enduring.

"Mindfulness is the practice of paying attention in a way that creates space for insight."

Sharon Salzberg

Insights & Individuality

Mindfulness will mean something different to each of us. I enjoy reading and listening to both Tara Brach and Lorin Roche yet their approaches are very different. Lorin emphasizes integrating mindful strategies into everyday life. His multi-sensory approach caught my attention keeping me curious about mindfulness. Tara's structured exercises and anecdotes are invaluable. Central to every approach to mindfulness is the focus on living in the 'present moment' and accepting life 'as it is'.

Go to one place, and really absorb it

'Exploring Venice' gives a structured framework for planning and enjoying your holiday in Venice. Simple strategies of mindful thinking and writing, giving stronger and more vivid memories. Finding a quiet place to sit at a cafe in a campo, jotting down brief details in a journal has a positive impact on wellbeing. Exploring the city with mindful attention means we notice the small details which would be usually be missed in the race to get to the next art gallery.

Creating stronger memories and connecting more closely with the essence of the place and people in a unique moment in time.

"You will realise the most curious thing in Venice is Venice herself"

Morris

Six Scenic Sestieri - Local flavours and atmospheres

The city of Venice has six sestieri. Each has an individual character.

Cannaregio: This is now the most populated Sestiere and has the border of the Fondamenta Nuove. The vibrant Cannaregio canal crosses through it with the Jewish Ghetto and historic Scuole and Churches like the Baroque Santa Maria Assunta, known as I Gesuiti.

Castello: historically the poorest district in eastern Venice with the Arsenale and the original cathedral of Venice - San Pietro. The views from the Riva near to Via Gariboldi are breathtaking on a sunny day. The Giardini in the far reaches of Castello houses the Biennale.

Dorsoduro: The Sestiere has a reputation as the artistic area. It is home to the Accademia and the Salute and Zattere. The name comes from the word for "hard ridge" as it was less swampy than other areas. The Giudecca Island is part of Dorsodura. In recent years its where I've spent my holidays in Venice as I discovered a Pensione with a garden which has drawn me back time after time.

San Polo: takes its name from the local Veneziana word for the church. It has the historic market and court area near the Rialto Bridge. You cross to San Marco over the Rialto bridge.

Santa Croce: the causeway joining Venice to the mainland - the Ponte della Libertà starts in Santa Croce. It has a lighter and more open character with some lovely campos where you can watch the world go by.

San Marco: is world famous and must be one of the seven modern glories of the world. It's where most people start their exploration of the city. The Piazza, the Basilica and the Doges Palace with the Bridge of Sighs. San Marco also has hidden areas around La Fenice and Santo Stefano towards the

Accademia Bridge. The main local 'high street' of shops begins in San Marco.

The house numbering system of Venice can seem very confusing when you are trying to find an apartment or small hotel in a calle. The houses are numbered not by street but for the whole Sestiere. An address may just be the building number within the Sestiere.

Routines & Rhythm of the City

Daily routines give a sense of serenity in a fast paced and often chaotic world. Even on a short vacation we quickly begin to form routines in the morning and evening. In a hot country there is the additional afternoon Siesta routine. You will start to tune into the rhythm of the city, maybe noticing the time when people go out and walk to a campo or Fondamenta to meet their neighbours or take an afternoon spritz.

Use the vacation to create routines purposefully, rather than them developing sporadically as they tend to at home. You may find a bar or café you like and return several times. You may find a route for an early morning walk which you return to more than once. Each day you will see something different even when you are walk the same route as the previous day. Make activities you enjoy into your Venice routine.

I was surprised to find how early in the evening Venice closes down, especially in the winter. By 9.30 p.m. many places are closed or closing. St Mark's Square is wonderful in the lantern light as is the walk along the Riva degli Schiavoni. There will be lots of options for an evening routine.

Mindful Moment ... Settle into your first Mindful Moment.

Momento di Mindfulness
'Wish you were here' exploring expressive writing

Take a walk and choose some postcards or special notepaper which appeals to you. Take inspiration from Pennebaker's work on expressive writing. Write yourself a postcard using the single word journal approach. Keep it short but write enough that reading the word will jog your memory and take you back in time to what you experienced. You could post it to yourself or just tuck it into the pocket of your suitcase where you will come across it in the future and remember the day.

If you enjoy writing then relax, reflect and write a letter to yourself. Write about your hopes for your holiday, any troublesome worries you have left behind, anything which has made you feel happy and contented. Put it in the envelope, address it to yourself and make a note to locate your letter and open and read it in six months' time.

Part 2

DAYBREAK & FIRST LIGHT

"A realist, in Venice, would become a romantic by mere faithfulness to what he saw before him."

Arthur Symons

Dreams on Waking

We dream while asleep but ... more importantly we should start each day with a dream. When on vacation it is even more important to spend time dreaming and then practically planning the day ahead. Before planning you need a gentle way to transition into the day. Feel the excitement and anticipation of a day exploring.

Begin the day with a Multi-Sensory Moment

Momento du Mindfulness
Transitioning into daytime

Choose an essential oil -maybe Rose Germanium, Cedarwood or Clary Sage.

If you are staying in a hotel and unable to use a traditional candle diffuser then just vaporise oil in hot water in the sink or use one of the new small re-chargeable aroma diffusers.

Experience the sensation of air flowing up your nostrils and down into your lungs. Make a brief purposeful pause before breathing out again. Pause at these 'points of turning' from one movement to another.

Allow your senses to 'sense' what is around you. Smell that essential oil in the burner. Moving smoothly into a mindful meditation.

Sit and let your gaze soften as if you are looking through half open eyes. Notice when thoughts wander in. Gradually those thoughts will disperse and dissolve. You've noticed, labelled them so they can shift to the far reaches of your mind.

Your mind will be settling. Smell the oil again. You want to reach the point where your mind is in the same state as when you are about to fall asleep. The difference is that you don't want to fall asleep this time and you want to stay very much awake.

Pay attention to your senses. Move your attention to different senses. Over time you will begin to notice your senses when you sit quietly this way.

Open Window - Venetian Soundscape
Wherever you are staying you will hear the unique sounds of Venice. The city has its own individual soundscape.

One room I've stayed in had the quietness of a garden view and the sound of birds. Another was right over a busy canal. From early morning the sound of the engines of the boats and occasional calls of the navigators. Contrasting soundscapes and both memories equally precious in their own way.

Wherever you are you will be able to tune into the sounds from your own particular open windows.

Momento di Mindfulness
Tune it to a Venetian Soundscape

Close your eyes for 3 minutes. Just be aware of the sounds you hear outside. Make a mental list of the sounds you hear. Your very own Listening List. Open your eyes and remember each of the sounds you heard.

New Day
It's a new day. Look at the light outside. It may be a sunny, dull or misty day. Venice is a city where artists praise the quality of the light. Breathe in the new light of this day – a holi*day*. One thing is 'clear as light' and that's that this new day will not turn out quite as expected. They never do – but why would we want that …

Early Morning Walk - Sensing the City
Take an early morning walk out into Venice. You don't need a plan for this. Just leave your hotel or apartment and walk. Stay aware of the quality of the light and whether it is a still or breezy day. Look around you at the buildings and the canals. Take in the varied Venetian colours. Use your senses to tune in to a multi-sensory Venezia. Here you are walking in the quiet early morning streets with background scenery which could be the canvas of a Renaissance artistic masterpiece. Today is still your own blank canvas. Start to notice the rhythm of the city

35

Punta Della Dogana

If I write about the walk out to the Dogana twice then it really doesn't matter as it will just reinforce the beauty of this walk. Dogana means Customs House and it's right at the far end of the island. The Dogana is now a contemporary art museum. At the end of the promenade the views of the Doge's Palace and Palladio's San Giorgio Maggiore are outstanding. This may be the best place in the city to take a photo. An early morning photo from the Dogana is a good start to the day.

Set off in the early morning. You can either walk along the Zattere or walk from the Salute to reach the Dogana. We usually walk along the Zattere as this catches the morning sunshine. You can walk a circular loop and start your walk on the Zattere going past the Dogana and ending at the Salute or vice versa.

Sometimes I prefer to keep in the sun's warmth and re-trace my steps back along the Zattere, perhaps stopping at a bar for an early morning cappuccino. You can walk all the way from San Basilio port to the Dogana at the end of the Zattere. Increasingly there are runners jogging past as well as a few dogs out for their early morning walks.

The Punta della Dogana building is triangular. It was the Dogana da Mar or maritime customs office. Merchandise and papers of ships were scrutinized here. The building was completed in 1682 by Giuseppe Benoni. The tower has two Atlases lifting a bronze sphere with Lady Fortuna on top. The statue turns like a compass in the wind to show wind direction. The building stopped being the customs house in the 1980s. It was abandoned for 20 years before being transformed into a contemporary art gallery. François Pinault gained a lease of 33 years and it is gaining a reputation as a gallery - in 2017 it hosted an exhibition of the work of Damien Hurst.

Fondamenta Zattere

The Zattere is a wide open space by the Giudecca canal. The Zattere stretches almost 2 kilometres. The name 'Zattere' means 'rafts' and refers to the merchandise (salt, coal and wood) which arrived here by rafts. It was originally called Fondamenta Carbonaria, referring to the coal. The Fondamenta has existed since 810 but the pavement dates from 1516.

I love the views over to Giudecca. The views across the canal are ever-changing, depending on the weather and the volume of traffic on the water. Along the Fondamenta there are cafes, restaurants, gelateria, a supermarket and more. It's a hive of activity. There is minimal shade so come prepared to protect yourself from the hot sun.

You pass La Calcina Hotel and Bar, where Ruskin wrote 'Stones of Venice' . You can have a drink or snacks on their pontoon terrace and gaze over to Giudecca.

You will walk past the Ospedale degli Incurabili, a large 16th century building which is now part of the Accademia. It was founded to help those with diseases like syphilis and then over time became an orphanage.

Momento di Mindfulness
Anchor a Moment

The word 'incurabili' brings to mind suffering and pain. Life is transient and there is always something to find to be grateful for, even when we might be in a dismal mood. On the Zattere it is difficult to feel miserable and it must be one of the top places in Europe to "live in the moment".

Tune in to compassionate thinking for the suffering of those who came to this 'hospital of the incurables'. Then think of something you have in your life (a person, place or skill) for which you are truly thankful. Keep whatever you are grateful for in your mind for a few seconds.

Then change tack and turn and look out towards the Giudecca and San Giorgio and feel anchored in this moment. Focus on the view, the temperature of the air, the sounds you hear and how your feet feel secure on the paving stones. This is a moment to anchor into your memory bank. Choose a small movement of your hands such as putting your thumb and finger together or holding one wrist with the other hand. Look again at the view. Then make the small movement with your fingers/hands again and anchor to the memory. Next time you make that small movement you should be able to recall the anchored memory and re-play and live in this moment again.

All the way along the Zattere you look across to Giudecca. You see the Molino Stucky Hilton (developed from a former flour mill), Zitelle Church, the unique Casa dei Tre Oci and the Redentore.

Venice was a key player in the salt trade. In the twelfth century the city had a monopoly. Trade stretched as far away as Alexandria. Salt was called the 'white gold' of Venice. You pass the old salt warehouses (magazzine del sale). These date from the 14th century. A more modern façade was added around 1830 by Alvise Pigazzi. The warehouses have the names of religious structures which were located closeby - so a link with history. They are San Gregorio, Trinitá, Gesuiti, Spirito Santo and Umiltá. The buildings are spacious and had to be to withstand the pressure of the condensation absorbing salt stored inside. The warehouses are now used for exhibitions and a boat repair shop.

Momento di Mindfulness
Re-tracing your Steps

Choose a street. Maybe it's the Fondamenta Zattere.
Re-visit & Re-trace your steps. Walk the same street twice.
Compare and notice different things each time you walk the street.

Vaporetto

[handwritten marginal note: Rainy Day Lines 4.1]

Many years ago my partner and I spent all afternoon on a rainy day on a vaporetto. It left San Marco and did a circle around Venice. We had to get off the vaporetto at the back of Venice at a windswept, deserted stop to buy another ticket. I remember using my learnt phrase at the kiosk and asking for "andate e return." Ticket in hand we changed boats and competed the other half of the circular tour. The boat actually went through the middle of the Arsenale which is no longer possible. It was spectacular and exciting to go through the actual middle of the historic Arsenale.

Nowadays this route would be Lines 4.1 and 4.2 which make a circular route around Venice. 4.1 is clockwise and 4.2 is anti-clockwise.

Other memorable vaporetto rides have been:

- going out past San Michele to Murano

- going past the railway station up the Cannaregio Canal and round the back of the port and up the Zattere
- out from the Zattere or Accademia, past San Marco and the Arsenale and on to Giardini before setting off the lagoon across to the Lido.

Memories of a very early morning ride from Accademia past San Marco and on to Giardini. It got more and more foggy as we approached the Arsenale stop. The boat was navigating by its radar. Suddenly the boat stopped as did all the boats around us. There was quite a group of boats gathered with engines stilled. Then out of the mist loomed an enormous cruise liner. It was invisible and then suddenly emerged from the mist.

My other memory is of travelling to the Lido on market day. The boat was busy with Venetians with shopping trolleys making their way to the market.

Mist and Fog
In the thick fog of the early morning, even in summer then the Vaporetto might need to navigate using its radar. Every vaporetto has a radar and you will see it if you look carefully at the roof of the captain's cabin. This explains why the Vaporetto idled while waiting for a cruise ship to appear out of the mist.

Momento di Mindfulness
Friendly Fog

Trust your own inner radar. Always be prepared to switch on loving 'kindness' and compassionate thinking when you need it.

The skill of being kind to yourself with self-compassion is difficult for many. Talk to yourself as your own best friend would. Treat yourself kindly. The tendency is for us to talk harshly to ourselves about something we have done or said. Yet so much in life is beyond our control.

Watch out for your own hyper critical 'inner voice' and how it speaks to you. It's a case of trusting that inner radar and tuning out the critical inner voice. Be warned – this inner voice can need a lot of training before it changes its tone.

Grand Canal

The Grand Canal follows a natural channel that travels in an S shape from the Bacino to Santa Chiara Church. It goes between two islands.

This long canal intersects with many smaller canals. A speed limit has been applied in recent years. Sometimes you hear a siren of a fire, police or ambulance boat. The Fire Station is just off the Grand Canal. Slower barges deliver goods or collect refuse. Sometimes a funeral barge can be seen on its way to San Michele cemetery.

The Grand Canal is lined with buildings from the 13th to the 18th century. Even the single storey modern looking Palazzo Venier dei Leoni housing the Guggenheim museum is much older than it looks. The first palazzos were working merchant houses with goods entrances and storage areas on the ground floor. The palazzos have gateways on the water and there are only a few Riva pathways lining the canal e.g. the Riva del Vino in San Polo. To see the Canal in its spectacular glory you need to travel by boat.

The restored Fondaco Dei Tedeschi is a new addition to the Canale scenery. This was historically where the German merchants had their central building. Now it is a department store with cafe. As you pass by, if you look up, you can often see people walking on the newly opened roof terrace. See the Palazzos Ca' Doro, Ca Rezzonico, Ca Foscari and the sublime Santa Maria della Salute. Pass under the Rialto Bridge and see the arches of the market area. Occasionally you may see a traghetto crossing the canal but these are rarer these days.

Take a Vaporetto like the Number 1 which goes all the way up the Canale. It's lovely to do this on the early morning of a hot summer day. Even in winter with mists creeping over the buildings you will see how the colours of the buildings merge into a renaissance palette of wintry colour.

Palazzos shimmer and shine with reflection from the water and the shape of the reflected buildings move in the water.

40

Momento di Mindfulness
Palazzo & Perspective

Palazzos on the Canale Grande have 2 entrances. A land and water entrance. The land and Canale entrance look very different. The land entrance may be down a dark Calle, hiding an internal courtyard and look nothing like a grand palazzo. The canal entrance will have a wide open and palatial appearance. Totally different.

Different perspectives. Consider how so many things can have a different perspective. So much in life can be seen from different perspectives. Spend a few minutes considering this is relation to your own life.

Four Bridges
The Grand Canal is punctuated by four bridges.

- Ponte dell'Accademia was built in the 1850s from steel but lacked stability. Later the bridge was built again with wood. It was meant to be temporary while a decision was made about the type of bridge to construct. The discussions continue more than 150 years on. It looks to have had something of a facelift in 2018 – it's looking good for its age.

- Ponte degli Scalzi connects the Santa Lucia railway station and Chiesa degli Scalzi (Church of the Barefoot Monks). It is 'The Bridge of the Barefoot'.

- Ponte Di Rialto will be covered in details in other sections of *'Exploring Venice'*. For many centuries this was the only bridge across the canal.

- Ponte di Calatrava or 'Ponte della Constituzione' is a modern glass bridge connecting Piazzale Roma with the railway station. It's the youngest bridge, opening in 2008 and still controversial

All of the bridges are unique in style and history. They give a good focus for walks when exploring the Grand Canal.

41

 *Momento di Mindfulness*
Bridging Across

Bridges integrate the city together. Building bridges. Bringing communities together.

Find and focus on a bridge. It doesn't matter which one. It could be the Rialto or a small bridge on a small canal. Take the opportunity to observe the design, materials which it's made out of and what it is joining together. Consider the details.

Stand on a bridge and look out and up a canal. Take a photo. Understand the uniqueness of the view you are seeing. Uniqueness in time and space. Stand solitary and serene, even if everything is busy around you. Stand still. Feel increasingly solitary and serene.

In the stillness of the day consider for a brief moment any bridges which you need to build with others. Someone you have lost touch with or where your communication isn't working very well at the moment.

Watching Working Boats
Where there is a lagoon there will be boats. This next section showcases some of the 'lagoon craft' you will notice as you explore the city.

Swish of the Oars
Watch out for a boat with one person rowing and the swish and grace of the oars. More often these days you will see a crew of 3 or 4 people rowing together, maybe practicing for the Vongalonga festival or just for the exercise and pleasure of being out on the water.

Drifting Dredgers
Attend to the different types of boats. There are many different kinds. My family often laugh at me as I have a fascination for watching a dredger at work, with its baskets of silt lifted up in a continuous rhythm. I've also watched the boats which carry the engineering 'kit' for sinking the wooden poles down into the lagoon - repairing and replacing the weatherworn poles. I notice the skill of the tug crew as they guide the behemoth of the cruise liners through the channel. The cruise terminal is being re-sited and you no longer see the large Greek

ferries which are already mooring at a different place away from the historic centre. The skill of the tug crew is very much needed and absorbing to watch.

Gracious Gondolas
Once we spotted an ancient covered Gondola in the Squero yard near San Trovarso. Watching the Gondolas being repaired or built in the boat yard (Squero) is a fascinating insight into artisan craftsmanship and history. The larger Traghetti are still to be found crossing the Canale Grande (though there are less of them and not every station is open these days) The wide and gracious traghetti gondolas are special.

Watching the Gondolas on the canal and manoeuvring in what looks like currents and tides of the Bacino is awesome. If you ever can manage to have a Gondola ride it is a unique way of seeing back canals and places where it is impossible to walk. I remember my parents finding a Gondola in a calle a long way from San Marco and negotiating a deal with the Gondolier and the excitement of a Gondola ride past Marco Polo's house.

Carrying People
Look out for the ACTV Ferry Boats and especially the Car Ferries making their way up the Giudecca Canal, out past the Dogana point and past San Marco. I've never been a passenger on one of those car ferries but I would like to do the journey. The island ferries are always there whatever the weather, bringing people to work in the morning and tourists visiting the islands later in the day.

Eco-Boats
I notice some boats are now part electric, like the Alilaguna transport boats from the airport to various points in the city. Often the boats sit low in the water - the Vaporetto and Alilaguna are low geared and low level boats.

Working Boats - now and then
On a morning the sound of the freighter boats supporting the road sweepers and refuse collectors who maintain the city streets every morning. The delivery boats - especially at Christmas time when they are piled full of boxes and deliveries to homes. Once we saw a flat platform with an attached engine taking a TV outside broadcasting van to San Marco ready for the visit of the Pope the next day.

The older working boats, like the Bragozza and the Sandalo with its sturdy flat bottom are the working boats of Venetian history.

Sometimes you may see a sailing ship in the distance - there is always something new to see.

 *Momento di Mindfulness*
Images of the Lagoon

Solitary island,

Ruined buildings

Mindful monastery

Subdued Shades

Defensive walls

Solitary Fisherman

Still lagoon

Harsh marshland

Lonely lagoon

Summer storm

In the air

Part 3

EARLY MORNING - SOON AFTER BREAKFAST

"his eye shifted to the façade of the <u>Basilica</u> and those absurdly asymmetrical cupolas, <u>the whole lopsided glory of it</u>. Brunetti stopped walking and put his hand up to quieten Vianello. In an entirely different voice, almost solemn, he asked, "We're lucky aren't we?"

Vianello glanced aside at Brunetti and then followed his gaze to San Marco and the flags whipping in the breeze, the mosaics above the door. The Inspector stood there for some time, looking at the church, then glanced to the right, across the water and towards San Giorgio with its ever-vigilant angel. In an entirely uncharacteristic gesture, Vianello raised his free arm and moved it in an arc that encompassed the buildings around them as well as those across the water, then he turned to Brunetti and patted his arm, quickly, twice. For a moment, Brunetti thought the Inspector was going to speak, but he remained silent and moved away towards the Riva degli Schiavoni and the sun-splashed walk down to the Questura"

'Suffer the Little Children' by Donna Leon

Angels on High

There is the Angel Gabriel on the Campanile, a host of six Angels accompanying Saint Mark, high up on the front façade of the Basilica and yet another 'ever-vigilant' Angel above the Campanile on San Giorgio. The city has a host of guardian angels. During Carnivale on the weekend before Shrove Tuesday there is now the 'Flight of the Angel' when an angel descends from the bell tower in the Piazza of San Marco.

Carni-vale

Reflective Reality - Mindful Mirror Day

On a sunny day you can see the reflections of the buildings merging into the green and blue glazed waters of the canals.

For a long time in European history all mirrors were made in Murano. Mirrors have a strange tradition and were seen as tools of the Gods. Roman mirrors were polished metal and the reality was that most people would only catch glimpses of themselves reflected in water. So when the Venetians began to make glass mirrors it gave a strange and new way of seeing your reflection. The creation of these Venetian mirrors came out of glass making. Glass makers discovered how to make a sheet of large crystalline glass with a reflective surface.

Murano became the centre of mirror making in the 1500s. Even when the secrets 'got out' and other places began to produce mirrors, the Venetian mirror was always special. Imagine a world when you never see your face or know how you look. Mirrored glass changed that forever.

Momento di Mindfulness
Mindful Mirror

There are many places where we catch a glimpse of our reflection when out and about during the day. Mirrors, windows, water, shiny metal surfaces.

Today notice when you catch a glimpse of your reflection. Use these times as a cue for your inner voice to say to you "I'm doing ok", Cultivating a supportive and not a critical inner voice is important for resilience in life. Taking a vacation is an important part of boosting resilience and 'bounce back' in energy levels.

Panoramic Sweep of Venice

The Riva degli Schiavoni is the most famous waterfront walk in Venice. It is both a promenade and a quayside. It's usually busy and at certain times of the day the section nearest to the Piazza can be overcrowded.

The Riva gets its name from Venice's Slavic merchant heritage. It was engineered during the ninth century and made from silt dredged from the lagoon. The promenade stretches from San Marco to the Arsenale where it changes to become the Rio Ca' di Dio. It eventually joins the Riva San Biasio which was added by Napoleon. This was the docklands area in medieval times with plentiful mooring for merchant ships.

At quieter times of year this walk along the Riva degli Schiavoni is one of my favourite walks. At busier times I prefer to 'promenade' at the other side of Venice along the Zattere. The Riva is always a lovely walk either very early in the morning or after sunset. Around Christmas there is a small children's fun fair with a traditional carousel with incredible painted animals.

Even if you visit in the height of summer you must do this walk along the Riva at least once. Once you have passed the postcard stands near the ACTV ferry terminal at San Zaccaria it gets quieter as you walk towards the Arsenale.

The view from Riva over to the island of San Giorgio and Palladio's elegant pillared, innovative structure alongside the old monastery buildings is breath-taking. Look the other way at the impressive architecture of the palazzos lining the Riva. Nowadays these are mostly hotels. Look at the different boats docked at the quayside.

When you walk past the Arsenale boat stop look to the left and you will see the Rio leading down to the Arsenale gates. Keep going straight on and then turn into Via Garibaldi where you can find somewhere to stop for a drink.

To Do

47

Momento di Mindfulness
Sunshine on the Riva

On a sunny morning in winter or spring walk up the Riva degli
Schiavoni past the Arsenale boat stop. In the early morning you should
have a quiet and easy walk along the Riva. Even later in the day the
crowds thin the further your walk from San Marco giving you a feeling
of space. The sea air is strong with negative ions.

Look out towards the island of San Giorgio. Sometimes it can look
hazy and distant. The lagoon in the Bacino looks turquoise and the sky
and water almost seem to merge together. The campanile of San
Giorgio stands out in the distance.

After misty days the sunshine can seem bright and this Riva is one of
the best places in the city to experience the warmth of the sun's
rays. There are benches here and you may be fortunate enough to be
able to sit and watch the world (boats in the Bacino) go by. Watch the
shapes and shadows of people passing by.

Spotlight on San Marco
Piazza San Marco, Doges Palace and Basilica

Here there are "lofty monuments and reflective soul"

Jan Morris

Every guidebook will have information about the specific sites and treasures of this area; the Piazza, the Doges Palace and the Basilica and its Campanile. Nowadays an online search should give a wealth of free information about St Mark's Square. Here the spotlight is still on key sights, but with a more mindful focus.

As you enter Piazza San Marco for the first time on any visit you have to pause. Just pause and have a 'freeze frame' moment. This elegant square was reputedly called the 'drawing room of Europe' by Napoleon. Just for today though it is your 'stage set' and you can make your own treasure trove of special memories.

Maybe you walk into San Marco from a narrow calle and suddenly find yourself in this contrasting wide open space with some of the most special, unique, architecture in history. Maybe you approach by boat, walking along the Riva degli Schiavoni and into the smaller Piazetta which leads into the main square. Suddenly you see the golden glory of the Basilica. It doesn't matter how you approach Piazza San Marco. Whichever way you will catch your breath at your first glimpse of this 'site of sites'.

If you are able to then visit very early in the morning and experience this place in quiet solitude, perhaps with an occasional 'piazza sweeper'. Come in the winter or early spring when this is a quieter place. Come in the late evening during the summer when the city is quieter.

You may have to just 'make do' with visiting on a busy summer afternoon if you are restricted to visiting just for a day. It is still worthwhile and you will just have to work harder at screening out the crowds which surround you.

Here you are in 'La Piazza'. It's the place to walk around and just gaze at what you see. Walk up the square while looking at the Basilica. If you are lucky the sun will be glinting on the gold of the mosaic frescos and the domes. Turn around and look at the Gothic Istrian stone buildings around the square. Look up. Gaze at the campanile and look at the saint and angelic figures perched on the top of the Basilica.

Pause at the Doges Palace. You have to. It's a Gothic Palace and seat of centuries of Venetian Republican power. There are stone arches and a covered portico at ground level.

50

Momento di Mindfulness
Arches in a Shady Arcade.

Wander into the shade of the Portico. There are stone benches under the arches at ground level with a loggia on the first floor above.

Simply walk slowly up and down the Arched Arcade noticing the details. Make sure you walk both ways (maybe several times) and keep paying attention to details on the stonework around you.

Look up at the ceiling of the passageway. The roof pattern is remarkable and absorbing in its structure. The ceiling arches are latticed and create an illusion of length and space.

If you are there at a quiet time of day and there aren't too many people around you can then gaze upwards and keeping walking slowly forward can be a very mindful meditational moment.

It costs nothing to wander into the lower courtyard and onto the impressive staircase leading up to the entrance to the Doge's palace. If *Inside* you want to explore further and go inside then there is an entrance fee.

Inside you can sit in the council chamber, see the Doge's apartment, view the artwork and experience the Bridge of Sighs from the inside and on to the desolation of the prison.

This was once the powerhouse of the Venetian Republic. With its Gothic detail, frescoed interiors and gilded ceilings you can feel the echoes of the power of the past.

Jan Morris describes sneaking onto the throne and the perspective of looking up at the frescoes on the ceiling. The Goddesses looking down in splendour from the ceiling of the Doge's Chamber. Jan Morris' escapade was in the twentieth century and is no longer advised!

The Palace has been destroyed by fire several times and re-built. It's a place which has seen sombre moments with news of Venetian defeats in Byzantium, despair about plague with a plea from the Council of Ten that a church would be built if the plague ended. Executions in the Piazza and torture in the prison.

Beware the Jaws of the Lion's

After a failed revolution in the 1330s the Council of Ten introduced a system of 'denunciation'. New lion's mouth mailboxes were set up across the city. They were placed in the walls of civic buildings and even church buildings. They appeared in every part of the city. Citizens were encouraged to make allegations of treason, criminal activity or immoral behaviour by posting a letter to the Council. The letter had to be signed and sometimes there might be a payment in order for the story to be investigated. The accused would be summoned and questioned and then there would be a vote to decide on guilt.
The penalty could be devastating; imprisonment, exile, galley slavery and occasionally death. This was a secret police approach to avoiding further dissent and the plotting of revolutions. It must have had the citizens always 'looking over their shoulders'.

As you walk past the Doge's Palace towards the lagoon this section of the Piazza is correctly known as 'the Piazzetta'. From the Piazzetta you see the Bacino of San Marco where the Grand Canal widens out into the lagoon.

On one side is the Biblioteca Marciano and on the other side are the Gothic arches of the Doge's Palace. As the Piazzetta meets the lagoon notice two granite columns. On top of these columns are statues of the two patron saints of Venice (these are copies with the originals in the museum). The lagoon waters used to come this far into the square and so these pillars gave a stately 'entry portal' from the sea to the city.

The first patron saint was Saint Theodore with his dragon (which actually looks rather like a crocodile) The other column has the winged lion representing Saint Mark, which it's thought may have come from Tarsus in southern Turkey).

It's said that in the early days of the Republic in the 13th Century that executions took place between these pillars at the symbolic point of this portal into the city.

The lion of St Mark is the symbol of Venice. Look out for other lions as you wander around San Marco Sestiere. There are other statues or carved images of lions on walls waiting to be found.

If you walk out from the square towards the San Marco vaporetto stop you will pass cafes and see the famous Harry's Bar. There is a small hidden garden close by which is being restored and many artist's easels and souvenir stalls. This area can be very hectic in the summer. At quieter times of the year it can be a pleasant extension to San Marco.

If you turn in the other direction at the two columns then you will cross a bridge and see the Bridge of Sighs before walking along the Riva degli Schiavoni.

The Piazza itself is a sort of elegant architectural 'drawing room'. In the evenings the combination of the lighting from the lamps and moonlight reflecting on the stonework give the Piazza a very different character.

Listen to the small orchestras playing outside the cafes in warm weather. The music is more noticeable in the evening. It is possible to walk and walk around this beautiful place and always noticing something different.

Café Society

For many years I resisted going into Florian's. Even though Caffè Florian's is in itself a museum, with links to the past, I always felt the cost of tea or Spritz was beyond my reach.

As a small child of seven on my first visit to San Marco I still remember my Grandma's stunned expression when she bought ice cream for my toddler brother at one of the cafes in the Piazza. He was tired, hot and fractious and Grandma did what grandparents do and ordered ice cream. It arrived in dishes with finger bowls served in pewter/silverware. My brother didn't even eat the ice cream; but the bill went down in family history as 'one of those memorable moments.' It took almost fifty years for me to venture into one of these cafes again.

I've often walked past Florian's and looked in the window - people watching. The decorations and frescos give it an especially inviting look on a cooler spring or winters day. This year on 'a whim on a winter's day' in late December we were wandering through the square when I suddenly said "Let's go to Florians" and we did. I took tea! With the hot water provided I made that drink last a very long time. The cake was a Zabbaglioni based confection and I took my time with that too - this might well have been a once in a lifetime experience. I recommend it if your budget will stretch to it - but regard it as an occasional treat. Donna Leon's Brunetti does call in here in one of the novels to meet a local doctor and that made me feel better about my extravagance. The furniture, the style, the friendly welcome made it a special experience on a cold, foggy December day.

Campanile

A Campanile has stood in the Piazza since the twelfth century and may have been a light house or watchtower in those early days. It's been re-built several times. Galileo used the campanile to study the skies in the early 1600s.

The Campanile collapsed on 14th July 1902. Nobody was hurt although a cat died in the rubble. After much deliberation the bell tower was rebuilt as a close copy of the collapsed tower. It took nine years for the copy to be built and the Angel was made from fragments of the original.

Nowadays it has robust, safe foundations and you can go by ~~To Do~~ lift/elevator right up to the top and see wondrous views of Venice, the wider lagoon and sometimes as far as the Dolomites.

This Campanile with a glimmering copper Angel Gabriel on top of a rotating platform has long been the first sighting of Venice for those arriving by sea. There is a 'flight of the angel' event as part of Carnivale on the last Thursday before Lent. An angel on a wire descends down from the Campanile for an awestruck crowd below.

The Basilica

I'm struggling with this section as the Basilica is such a visual spectacle that it is very hard to describe in words. It's just an amazing sight. Its five domes rise up above the square. The building is embellished with glinting, gleaming, glorious, golden Byzantine mosaics. The golden decoration is both outside on the facade of the building and inside the domes. Many of the mosaics are from the thirteenth century and some possibly go as far back in time as the third century. It is known locally as the Basilica d'Or.

San Marco only became the main cathedral of Venice in 1807. It feels Eastern and the influence of Byzantium in obvious in its domes. Records have the Basilica consecrated in 832 when it became the place to shelter the remains of St Mark.

The main dome is called the Ascension dome and this is covered with early thirteenth-century mosaics. The mosaics in the church's Atrium are made of small glass pieces combined with gold leaf.

St Mark is buried within the altar, surrounded by marble and alabaster columns. The golden altar screen is a jewelled treasure. Legend tells us that St Mark did visit the lagoon. However his body didn't always rest here. His remains were stolen from Alexandria in around 828. Some Venetian merchants hid the relics in barrels of pork, knowing that the Muslim guards would not touch the pork allowing them to escape back to Venice.

The voyage back was eventful with the ship almost sinking in a storm, until the spirit of San Marco spoke to the captain and told him to take down the sails. This story sequence is shown in mosaic above the left door of the main entrance.

The four famous gold-plated bronze horses were taken from the Hippodrome of Constantinople during the Fourth Crusade. Copies of the horses stand on the front balcony of the Basilica. If you pay a small fee you can go and stand on this loggia and look down on the square and out over the city.

So the Basilica is unique and glistens and glitters even on a cloudy day. This was the Doge's private chapel and he even had his own pulpit within the Basilica. The building was decorated over the early years of the Republic with treasures which the merchants found on their voyages. A unique building with and an incredible atmosphere.

We'd walked through San Marco Piazza on Christmas Eve before and seen the long snake of a queue stretching from the Basilica right across the length of the Piazza. This year we walked past just as the end of the queue was going in for the Christmas Eve service. On an impulse we quickly joined the end of the queue and went in to the Basilica for the service. We found a stone seat to sit on just inside the main door. It was a true experience. The golden roof was captivating in the lamplight. The music and Latin/Italian voices took us back to another era. In contrast to this the local people kept coming in and walking past us, staying for just a short time. Often there were strollers and small children giving us a very modern scene of Venetian life.

Previously we have tried to visit the Basilica at dusk. There are often fewer visitors at the end of the day as the church gets ready to close its heavy doors. You may even feel you almost have the place to yourself. The fading sunlight catches the precious mosaics with gold leaf giving a luminous golden illumination. Book in advance online and you will not have to queue for very long.

o Book line
or line

 Momento di Mindfulness
Types of Treasures:

Tune in to surroundings. Stay focused
Peaceful place with echoes of the past.
Notice dimly lit spaces.
Gleaming, golden mosaics.
Precious coloured jewels,
Treasure of ancient centuries.
Consider the types of treasures in life
What do you treasure?

Ponte dei Sospiro ... or the Bridge of Sighs.

"Many an innocent man to walk the Bridge of Sighs and descend into the dungeon which none entered and hoped to see the sun again."

'Innocents Abroad' by Mark Twain

Ponte dei Sospiri has a reputation for being a historically haunting, melancholy place. This is more than a bridge, it's actually a covered walkway. Starkly elegant and made of grey limestone and designed by Antonio Contino. Construction began in 1600 and has a definite Venetian Baroque style.

There are actually two views of the bridge. The most famous view is from Ponte della Paglia on the Riva on the southern side. Ponte Canonica on the northern side is more shadowy, giving a quieter and less crowded viewpoint.

If you are in the Doges Palace and looking out from the inside of the corridor then take your time as you look through the small latticed window in the middle of the bridge. This is the poignant moment when condemned prisoners sighed as they looked at their last view of the Lagoon. Casanova stood here 1755 and spent 15 months in prison before his spectacular escape.

Momento di Mindfulness
Breathe & Sigh

It's the 'world famous" Bridge of Sighs so the Mindful Moment has to be one of the cornerstones of mindfulness. Breathe and Sigh.

Breathe…Sigh…breath
Look at the Bridge
Close your eyes
See the image of the bridge in your mind.
Breathe … Sigh… breath again
Look at the Bridge again
Feel gratitude for your freedom today

A Moated City - Refuge in Rivo Alto

Venice began as a refuge, a haven from the conflict and devastation in the surrounding countryside. In the early days safety was a priority with the fortified watch towers giving people an early warning when it was necessary to move even further into the murky, misty lagoon.

The largest moat ever with no need to build walls for self-defence. The walls which were built were stately Palazzo warehouses. People adapted to living in a watery, moated city. They survived and then they thrived.

Malamocco was the original capital and that settlement eventually disappeared into the sand. The site of Malamocco is near to one of the entry points from the Adriatic into the lagoon. You see the name Malamocco on one of the car ferries. Torcello was also a sizeable, influential settlement which seems to have been reduced to oblivion by malaria.

Rivo Alto changed from being a 'haven' to becoming the main centre; the place where people lived and traded to make a living. The pronunciation of Rivo Alto becoming condensed (as words tend to be in the dialect of Veneziano) to 'Rialto'.

The city became solid and successful. The living 'defensive moat' worked practically when Pepin's invading fleet was defeated. The Genoese struggled to find their way out of the lagoon once they realised they were in serious trouble. All signs of shipping channels and safety had been removed. The ships were unable to locate Venice and then floundered while the seaweed swayed around them. Legend has it that an elderly woman told the invaders to go 'straight on' … 'dritto, sempre dritto' and this led to their doom.

Rialto Bridge & Beyond

Rialto is more than a bridge. Rialto is an area of Venice and the heart of the ancient trading republic of Venice. It was in Rialto that merchant adventurers traded goods from the East. It was here that merchants would meet to talk, swap stories of their trading voyages. It was here that plotting and planning for new voyages happened.

I always imagine the Rialto area as the stage set for the Shakespeare play 'The Merchant of Venice'. It is an atmospheric area with the bridge steps in the background. So you need to spend a couple of hours looking at the highlights of Rialto.

Whichever side you approach Rialto from it will be busy. The major Italian shopping streets with department stores like Coin and the newer Fondaco dei Tedeschi are very close to Rialto.

If you walk from San Marco to Rialto it can almost feel as though you are on the verge of being crowd surfed by those following the well-worn path from one key site to another. If you approach from the market side of the Canal the streets will be noticeably busier as you approach Rialto.

I'm going to assume you reach Rialto from the San Marco side of the canal. You are almost at the Rialto Bridge when you reach a small campo with shops, some souvenir stalls and a public toilet. Get your bearings. Look around and imagine the people in Medieval or Renaissance costumes instead of modern dress. Often walking tours start somewhere near this place. There are many Vaporetto stations and so you can always escape quickly from the crowds if you need to.

Everyone should go under the Rialto Bridge, so at some point you need to take one of those vaporetti along the Grand Canal and sail under the Rialto Bridge.

Momento di Mindfulness
Crowd Coping Strategies

It is when I am queuing or in a crowded place that mindfulness has made a noticeable difference to my personal coping levels. Now, if I am in a lengthy queue I purposefully close my eyes briefly, then let my gaze soften and zone out. It gives me a moment of mindfulness in what was previously a trigger for irritation and temper.

If I walk through San Marco, along the Riva or take the route from San Marco to Rialto I do the same. I focus on my footsteps and zone out from the people about me. Of course I still look where I am going!

Start by briefly closing your eyes. Then focus on your breathing. If you are in a queue then focus on an object close-by, even just part of a bag. Just keep breathing at a slower rate. This is almost like being in a trance, but you are consciously moving forward and aware of everything around you.

When you are in a press of people in a crowd then it is important to breathe, think to yourself 'this is as it is and it will be over soon' and keep moving forward. It would be difficult to 'zone out' in a crowd but it is just about possible to close out some of the noise and background bustle. Focus on moving forward while keeping calm and focused.

Crowd coping strategies work if you 'work at them'. It is an acquired skill but it is one which is worth cultivating. This is about tolerance and intolerance. It is powerful to use the mindfulness strategy of 'acceptance' when in these sorts of situations. This is *'as it is'* and I can't change it this minute and I notice that I feel tired, fed up and frustrated but that means I'm giving unnecessary energy to those emotions. This is a time to accept and just move on (literally). After moving on from the feeling of irritation and frustration you can cope until the crowds thin.

View from the Bridge
The Rialto Bridge was first opened in 1591 and is probably the most famous and most visited bridge in Europe. Since the 12th century, a number of wooden bridges have been built in this same place. The bridge is built of the typical white Istrian stone seen throughout Venice.

Move towards the bridge and climb the stairs. In true merchant adventurer inspired style there are shops built into the middle of the bridge. The marble steps have been restored in the last couple of years, in fact the whole bridge has been given a 'face lift' courtesy of the fashion house Diesel. Now as an adult I am a little 'snobby' about the shops. However tucked away in my treasures at home is a small decorated purse on a golden chain which I chose as a child at a souvenir shop towards the top of the steps on the bridge. Those shops still glisten with jewels and gold in a way that has strong roots in past history.

Once at the top you can move out from the shops towards each side of the bridge. And the view. You can look in either direction and you should. Today you are probably one of many tourists trying to take their 'definitive snap' on Rialto Bridge.

Take your time. I actually think that in a strange way we all need to experience the Bridge when it is busy, exhausting and vibrant with people. Then I think we all need to experience it in the early morning sunlight and again after dark when it is illuminated by soft lamplight and perhaps moonlight. At each times of the day you will find a different Rialto Bridge.

Momento di Mindfulness
Taking Steps on the Rialto Bridge

Focus and make this experience last. Hopefully you are visiting when it is quieter. If not, then never mind, it will still be a special moment.

Link back in your thinking to those who have used this bridge over the centuries. Find the view from the bridge out over the Canal whenever you can. If you walk along the edge rather than up the middle between the row of shops you will keep getting glimpses of the Grand Canal.

Stand somewhere and separate yourself out from the crowds. This may take some mental agility but it will be worth it. Separate out and find a moment of inner silence. Look out at the view. Maybe go to the other side and do the same looking down at a different view.

Feel thankfulness for life and being 'here in this moment'. Many never will. This is a privilege. Feel this link with history. Mindful Gratitude for today.

To Market Venetian Style

Walk down the bridge into the market area. This area is usually bustling. As a small child my parents always brought us here when we were on a day trip to find a stall selling chips which was always round the side and not far from the foot of the bridge. How dreadful you may say ... but those chips were anticipated with excitement and we would have been unable to afford a cafe or restaurant.

You need to take in the Magistrates Court, which is a lovely building and the unusual clock looking down on the market.

Pescheria and the Erbaria

Explore the fruit and fish markets. As you wander through you get glimpses of the Grand Canal. Stalls on the fish market are lined green, damp and cool filled with the colours of glistening fish. Vegetable stalls are piled high with seasonal produce.

Nowadays there are fewer stalls and the Venetians are concerned at this year on year reduction. Even with the rise in self-catering accommodation the local market doesn't seem utilised by those visiting for vacation. That seems such a shame and if you are self-catering then consider getting into the daily routine of visiting the Rialto market.

The fish and fruit/vegetable markets are separate and housed within what feels almost like medieval cloisters. It can be surprisingly quiet on an afternoon after the stalls have packed up and you can wander amid an occasional carrot or artichoke peeling and find yourself almost alone.

I have a dream that one day I will spend a month or more in an apartment in Venice and visit the market every morning to buy produce and then cook for lunch or dinner. I've mentioned Donna Leon's Brunetti novels several times and the Brunetti family plan their meals by what is in season at the market. Paula Brunetti will come here on a morning and 'weigh up' what is on offer. A topic of conversation around their dinner table might be the sight of a vegetable or fruit arriving because it is now 'in season'. Courgette flowers or white asparagus perhaps. Sometimes Guido Brunetti will walk home via the market and see something on a stall and buy on impulse. Daily, sustainable local produce leading to creative seasonal menus.

Momento di Mindfulness
Take Tea

Close to the market and towards the Grand Canal you will find a couple of bars facing the canal. Swing round past the fish market and come across the view. In warmer weather you can find tables outside.

There are bars here and once my sister-in-law spotted Francesco Da Mosta, who is a famous Venetian who a few years ago made a series of programmes about Venice for the BBC. These programmes are definitely worth searching out on DVD. My sister in law noticed Francesco leaving one of the local bars after having a coffee.

You really are in the heart of Venice. It is encouraging to know that it is still an important place to the Venetians and they continue to claim it 'as theirs' despite the volume of tourist traffic passing through the area every day.

A couple of years ago I spent a good hour sitting outside one of these bars with a pot of herbal tea, watching the canal and life around me. A pot of tea is wondrous for these times as the cup can usually be refilled 2 or 3 times. Choose lemon if you are having plain 'English Breakfast type' tea and drink it very weak. As a hot drink it can be surprisingly refreshing.

In the same way as for the 'raisin exercise' (which is integral to any introductory mindfulness text or course) make each step of the process of drinking tea into a mindful moment. Instead of the sequence being automatic make it into a conscious experience. From holding the cup, to raising it to your lips, to initiating a swallow and feeling the swallow happening. Work through each step of the sequence with 'slow motion thinking'. Moving from automatic to conscious thought is integral to daily practical mindfulness.

Bacaro
I think some people may walk across the bridge and continue in a straight line to San Polo and miss exploring the market area more fully. Miss the market cloisters which border the Canal. Or fail to notice the

Market Square clock with its unique hands representing the golden sun.

The area just past the market has started to become quite trendy in the last few years due to word spreading through books like Russell Norman's '*Polpo: A Venetian Cookbook (of Sorts)*' highlighting the traditional Bacaro and Cicchetti. Bacaro were the traditional working class wine bars, where for lunch or a light snack you can find a range of Cicchetti. Each Cicchetti is a small sized, 'flavour packed' couple of mouthfuls with a range of individual and delicious toppings. Fennel, artichoke, olives, redcurrants, walnuts on cream cheese, tuna, cuttlefish. The range is endless and individual to each bar. Traditionally Cicchetti are taken with a small glass of wine (un ombra). This might be the unbottled Veneto red or white wine.

There is more on Chiccetti in other sections of this book. However in this part of Rialto you may well stumble across the small All' Arco or the Da Mori Bacaro. Da Mori dates back to 1462. It's panelled with dark stained wood and copper pots and pans hanging down from the ceiling.

Sometimes a vacation transforms what we eat at home. We now have a Cicchetti inspired meal a couple of times a month. I admit to veering from tradition from the flat Veneto wines and having sparkling Prosecco with my developing range of home-made Cicchetti. My inspiration is a book called '*Venice: Recipes Lost & Found*' written by Katie and Giancarlo Caldesi and my little white bread rolls are gradually improving. They resemble a Focaccia recipe with the addition of olive oil to the recipe and are the perfect base for a cream cheese and walnut crostini.

I've noticed that you can now book a walking tour which takes you to several 'Cicchetti bars'. This may be an easier way to explore this area of Rialto and the Bacaro. It depends how long you have in the city and if you can afford it then a walking tour of the Bacaro may be an easy way of experiencing this local tradition.

Little Giacomo - the oldest church in Venice?

As you walk away from the Rialto Bridge into the market watch out for the Church of San Giacomo di Rialto. The locals call it 'Little Giacomo'. It is rather beautiful. It is one of the oldest, if not the oldest, church in Venice with some saying that parts of it date back to 420

AD. It was certainly mentioned in manuscripts as existing in the tenth century.

Look out for the writing on the six columns of marble as these characters have been dated to the 11th century. The columns may be originally from Ancient Greece. The building mostly survived the Great Fire of Venice which destroyed most of Rialto in 1514. Little Giacomo was restored to continue as a backdrop to the trading activities of the merchants in the market place of the re-built Rialto.

The Gothic portico gives the church a definite Roman feeling. It almost resembles a Roman villa. It is in the shape of a cross topped by a central dome which gives it that Byzantine element. This church really is a mix of different centuries of architectural style. The clock has an unusual face, based on the 24 hour clock, with hands representing golden sunshine. I love it.

Apparently the clock has never kept good time. How many merchants have been late for meetings by relying on this strange clock? Some say even the clock dates from the fifth century; but no one can confirm that.

Momento di Mindfulness
Mark the Moments of the Day

Look up at the golden sunshine marker of the clock. Imagine time passing through the centuries and this may be the oldest clock in the city. No wonder if it is tired and loses a little time. Think slow motion thoughts as you gaze at the stonework and the design of the clock.

The sun shines on the Roman numerals and the sunshine hands of the clock. Take a photo or find a photo or postcard of the church clock to keep. In the future you could choose a day when you work through the hours while referring to an image of this ancient clock. Stare at the symbolic golden sunshine which mark the hours of the day.

A Shoppers Paradise?
If you continue from the market area towards the signs for Accademia then look out for the church of San Giovanni Elemosinario. This is a mindful way to end your visit to the Rialto area. You hardly notice the

66

entrance. We walked past it several times struggling to find it as the entrance is between two shops. It is truly embedded in the merchant quarter of Venice. This church was closed for restoration and reopened in 2002. You can pause to look at art on the altarpiece by Titian. There seems agreement this isn't Titians finest work but it is worth a look.

Enter through a gated entrance, which is nothing like a usual church entrance. If you find this church then you can spend a few minutes of quiet meditation taking in the peaceful atmosphere while being so close to one of the busiest tourist areas in the world. So busy a place in fact that in 2018 the Mayor trialled turnstile barriers to limit the number of visitors causing some international attention.

Momento di Mindfulness
Seeking Serenity at Elemosinario

This is a place for shoppers to come in and light a candle and make a prayer. You are in the heart of the local community. You enter the church from the middle of a row of shops - it truly is a shopper's church. In winter feel the inevitable chill and smell of damp and in summer feel the welcome cool of the stonework.

Find a pew and sit and look around the church at the stonework and paintings.

Christmas in Rialto
If you visit around Christmas or in the months leading up to Carnival in February then you will see the strings of decorative lights stretching across the Rialto market and bridge. A sparkling pathway from one part of Rialto to another. This is a beautiful, spectacular sight.

Return to Rialto
You need to visit the Rialto Bridge more than once. Try to return in the early morning before most hotels have served breakfast. You will still find people busy setting up the area and the boats starting their day's rounds. This is the time of day to hop on a vaporetto at Rialto and see the Grand Canal. Or if you enjoy walking then go on a circular tour which takes in Rialto Bridge, through San Polo to the Accademia. You can stop there or continue on a longer route through Santo Stefano and close the loop by going back round again to Rialto. At certain times of the day this route would take you hours, but first thing in the morning you will be able to walk freely and take in the sights and sounds of Venice.

Momento di Mindfulness
Memories of a Spring Walk

We took this walk from Rialto through San Polo to the Accademia some years ago in March. It was about 8.00 a.m. and raining when we set off from our hotel in the San Marco Sestiere, but the sun came out as we made our way over the Rialto Bridge and through the market area.

The pavements glistened with raindrops on the paving stones. I remember seeing the Wisteria, early in flower clambering over crumbling brick walls. I remember hearing the sounds of children on their way to school in ancient palazzo buildings. Make sure you remember your own walk so you can think back and remember it when you are back home again.

I took photos on our walk. It was easy to snap the buildings and views from the bridges as we were often the only people there. I still have those photos saved and it only takes a glance at them for me to trace the memories of my steps on that spring walk from Rialto to the Accademia.

Souvenir Shopping at Rialto

The authentic market experience is a priority. However I'm going to mention the 'tourist type' market shops. Although the stalls are full of merchandise from the modern far east there is something compelling about 'Gift and Souvenir' shops, especially for children. I remember buying a pen which had a gondola moving up and down, a Gondolier doll and when I was much older a set of colourful champagne flutes. The glasses were inexpensive and unlikely to have been made in Venice, but I bought them and have kept them because they always remind me of a happy day in Venice. This is why we have souvenirs. If you do wish to 'surf the souvenir shops' then the shops joining the 'market proper' are as good a place as any to browse.

Momento di Mindfulness
Comedy as Art – Happy Harlequin and Pensive
Pierrot

The character of Harlequin in his checked costume may possibly have
originated from Venice. '*Arlecchino*' is a comedic servant character
from the *Commedia dell'arte*. Harlequin is a happy and clever character
who thwarts his master's romantic plans while pursuing his own love
for Columbina. Harlequin is often seen competing with the more
serious and melancholy Pierrot. It is no surprise that the word 'zany' is
a Venetian word.

Harlequin is traditionally a devilish character in Medieval mystery
plays, especially French plays. Maybe he did originate in Venezia as he
is often masked.

Consider the contrasting emotions represented by the two characters
Harlequin and Pierrot. Harlequin is fun loving and funny whereas
Pierrot is serious and sad. How do you relate to the emotions?
Happiness and Sadness at opposite ends of a continuum. Consider
what has made you feel happy, made you smile and what has made you
feel pre-occupied with cluttered thoughts.

Giudecca Market Stall

Morris describes Giudecca as full of flower and vegetable gardens and calls these 'small bowers of delight'.

The Women's Prison on the Giudecca island has a growing reputation for the quality of its market garden produce. The fruit and vegetables are sold to customers on Thursday mornings by women from a stall on the Fondamenta just outside the prison.

The Rio Terà dei Pensieri Co-operative supports skill development and the re-introduction of prisoners into the community (see reference section). It's first project began in 1994 and was to create a Garden of Wonders within the old garden of the Convertiti convent which houses the Women's Prison. Other craft and artisanal projects are now established and overseen by this co-operative organisation.

Wisteria And Sunshine

A spring walk through San Polo and Dorsoduro gives a glimpse of gardens and greenery through iron gates and over stone walls. The Magnolia is in flower. Wisteria vines curl and creep over buildings.

'Wisteria & Sunshine' for an Enchanted April in Italy (*the novel by Elizabeth Von Arnim is set in Italy in springtime and is my favourite novel and movie*)

Any Sestiere of Venice will have hidden gardens. Throughout Venice you will find signs of green spaces and secret gardens.

Wisteria and Magnolia are very Venetian plants. Magnolias are tall and visible and Wisteria climbs high over houses. Both give colour and shade in the spring time. Look out for these two complimentary plants as you walk through the quieter streets of Venice.

Momento di Mindfulness
Climbing & Trailing Pathways

Look out for unkempt gardens with plants trailing over walls and scrambling over buildings. Gaze at the foliage and any flowers. If you are lucky you might catch a scent of Jasmine in the summer as you pass a hidden garden.

Life might be compared to the analogy of a climbing, trailing plant. Growing in spurts and extending rapidly, then some frosty times with risk of blight. The need to keep some shape and order and the human desire for control (pruning).

Ivy is a plant which is tenacious, strong with its dark green foliage. Although never the most popular of plants it is usually there in shady places and grows in poor soil when facing hardship. Strong roots and anchoring itself to buildings. If one part is pulled back then another will still keep growing. Sometimes in life we need the resilience and strength of Ivy to bounce back from difficult times.

Focus and de-cluttering our lives is rather like pruning and training a plant. This can be a hard pruning or a light gentle trimming. It's hard to see clearly where to go next when surrounded by considerable clutter.

Powerful Palazzos
Gothic Golden Grandeur - Marbled Magnificence at Ca D'oro
Gothic style is individual. Ca D'oro is a frothy, wedding cake of a building. When first built it was covered in patterns with gold leaf paint. It isn't in a strict architectural style and has been embellished over time as fashions changed. Starting with a Medieval Byzantine template, Gothic features were added and it merges together harmoniously.

This was Gothic when it was new and 'cutting edge'. When Gothic started to first appear, Venice's Palazzos were already influenced by Byzantine eastern places. Gradually Byzantine became Gothic and the face of the city changed. In Ca D'oro Gothic arches with pointed ends are shaped by an eastern curve. You catch site of its Gothic arches from across the canal. It's magical when the light reflected from water bounces off the Istrian stone window frames.

Ca' Doro was the home of the Contarini family and it was their "golden house". They traded in spices, fabrics and dyes. The golden decorations when it was shiny and newly built have been eroded by weather and salty air. The palazzo has a feeling of space created by its 350 square metres of internal courtyard. This courtyard is a work of art with precious marble worked into complicated geometric patterns. Greens, reds and yellows in patterns resembling Roman mosaics.

Ca' Doro has been an art gallery since the Francetti art collection was given to the government in 1916. However the true experience is the building and the views from the enclosed balcony or loggia of the main salon. Wander and experience the link with the people living at the height of the power of the Venetian Republic.

Don't lean on the balcony. My mother did this some years ago, drawn in by the views across and several attendants immediately rushed in her direction asking her to stand back.

Momento di Mindfulness
Cool Courtyards

While walking in Venice on a hot day you might notice a cool courtyard.

Glimpses of courtyards, green leaved gardens, stone wells and internal stone staircases.

Silent, Peaceful, Still Spaces,

Stop and be still
Notice your thoughts
Step outside of emotions
Pause your breathing
Breathe out on a sigh
Give attention to breath
Calm Conscious Control
Of breathing
Engage and Gaze
Experience this moment

If it is Biennale time (either art or architecture) then many of the Biennale Fringe Pavilions are situated in historic palazzos and often have free entrance. This is a fantastic way to experience more of the secret history of the city. Wandering in and viewing the art display and the interior of a Palazzo and the views from its windows at the same time.

Position is Everything - Ca Foscari
The other Palazzo spotlighted in this section is on the other side of the
Grand Canal. Sometimes Ca Foscari has free entry. We've been lucky
enough to explore it during the Biennale and also on a specific night in
the summer where all the art galleries and museums were free just for
an evening. This Palazzo is the heart of the university - the Ca Foscari
University.

During the same period that Ca D'oro was being built the Foscari's
built their own imposing Gothic palace. No Golden House here - this is
simply Casa Foscari or House of the Foscaris. The position is
spectacular on the wide, central curve of the Grand Canal. Position is
everything. You can stand gazing out at the Grand Canal. It is a
precious viewpoint.

Here you can touch the cool, smooth marble as you wander through the
building. Mindful Marbles contrasting with a hot summer's day.

Film set favourite - Palazzo Dandalo (Danielle Hotel)
One of the most famous Gothic palaces in Venice is the Palazzo
Dandolo on Riva degli Schiavoni. This palace was built for the noble
and powerful Dandolo family. It has a beautiful facade and blends well
with the Doge's Palace which is pretty much next door. It's a film set
and appears in movies like "Only You' and 'The Tourist".

In 1822 the palace became the Hotel Danieli with luxurious internal
fittings. Famous guests have included Dickens, Goethe, Byron,
Benjamin Britten, Wagner, Bernstein and with a nod to its movie set
fame both Spielberg and Harrison Ford. Some like Ruskin have written
while staying there. Ruskin was working on The Stones of Venice
while in residence. George Sand (Aurore Dudevant) stayed here with
Alfred de Musset.

I've never been inside but have looked through its revolving doors and
in the darkness of winter seen glimpses of colourful furnishings and
chandeliers which mean this entrance could almost be a portal back in
time.

I'm not commenting on the ugly extension called the Danielle Excelsior
- some things are best left unmentioned.

Seaweed and Algae

All along the canals at intervals there are steps down to the water. Nowadays they are often covered with fronds of seaweed and what looks like green algae, so the steps have become green and slippery. The seaweed fronds float out in the water.

Seaweed and algae are living in difficult, aversive environment with the diesel from passing boats. There is an environmental issue here as in the past the canals wouldn't have been choked by seaweed. However the seaweed and algae are resilient in adverse conditions surviving and living in a potentially polluted ecology.

Momento di Mindfulness
Mini Break Silent Mantra

While wandering round on your first days in the city spend some time thinking of your 'mindful mantra' for your time in Venice. Consider choices while you are taking in the sites, the colours, the reflections of the buildings in the lugubrious green-blue canals.

Find a short phrase linked to the city which you can call up and think of while sitting for a few minutes. Maybe it is 'lugubrious lagoon' or 'Serene Serenissima'. It doesn't matter as it just needs to be something which means something to you and which you can remember.

This is a silent meditation. You can say your 'mindful mantra' to yourself when you need to reduce the volume of any stressful thoughts. Your mini break silent mantra.

Part 4

MID MORNING

"Beauty of surface, of tone, of detail, of things near enough to touch and kneel upon and lean against."

Henry James

Chorus Churches

If you are on a budget and looking for a way to gain entry to a number of ancient monuments then the Chorus Pass is definitely worth considering. The Chorus pass gives you entry to a range of churches across the city.

It's possible to plan a 2 or 3 day itinerary visiting churches in the different Sestiere of Venice. We started doing this when visiting Venice one March whilst on a tight budget. The churches gave an insight into the different periods of history and are often art galleries and architectural splendours in themselves. At each church you get a Guide Sheet with basic information which is more than enough to navigate round the building and not miss anything.

Often I would wander around and find a pew and sit and look around the building. My partner would instead look around with very specific focus on each painting. I have to say that after walking on paving stones it was nice to be able to sit down for a short time and focus on the overall style of the building.

Sometimes a pillar, a lectern or a vaulted ceiling would catch my interest. Sometimes it would be a window and the pattern of light in the building. Sometimes the art work would be my focus. The story and the background to the painting. The renaissance costumes in a biblical scene and my wondering about the faces depicted. Had the artist modelled these on people he knew - we know this often happened and it does give the art work an added human dimension.

There are usually about 18 Chorus churches to visit and if one of the churches is not available due to restoration then Chorus puts in a substitute. Tickets can be purchased either in some Churches or at the Tourist Information Office close-by San Marco.

The Chorus website gives clear opening times and any closures. The cost at time of writing in April 2019 is 12 euros per person, a family card costs 24 euros and there are reductions for students up to 29 years of age. If you only have a short time then each church can be visited individually for 3 euros. The Chorus Pass lasts for 12 months.

78

Momento di Mindfulness
Find your Focus

Each church you visit will be unique. Walk in and simply walk around
and look at the features of the building. Something will catch your eye.
Follow and focus on '*that something*'. It might be a colour or an image.
It might be the pattern of sunlight shining through glass or alabaster. It
might be the glinting of a gold mosaic. It might be carved stonework. It
might be a candle in a side chapel.

Find and focus on one single aspect of the church. Look again and look
differently. Noticing a detail. Close out other stimuli around you. You
are single channelled and focusing fully on your choice of object.

Commit it to memory. You are making your own Chorus Collection.
Each individual item will form a Chorus Line in your minds memory.

Sit quietly, whatever your faith, and connect with the ancient spiritual
essence of the place. Feel your feet on the floor and focus inwards.
Find a connection with bygone centuries and people who lived and
worshipped here.

A moment of connection and yet separateness from their world.

'Connection and Separateness' is a theme throughout Venetian history.
In Venice the city was built by refugees making a life away from
conflict and continual fear of invasion. The lagoon gave a protective
shield and helped those people develop an independent style of
thinking. The islands of Venice developed structure and the splendid
buildings grew into a city.

Churches were built and embellished over time with marble, precious
treasures, relics and art work. People separated from the mainland had
survived and formed a new community. Venice became a City
Republic separate from neighbouring states. La Serenissima was
powerful in its separate identity.

'Space and separateness' yet with people developing strong
connections and community identities.

Calm in a Cloister

Walk in a Cloister
If you visit Venice on a warm day in late spring or during the heat of summer then consider spending a morning exploring those churches which have a cloister. Most of the time we stumble across a cloister attached to a church and it's a hidden surprise. However because walking in a cloister can be a truly mindful experience why not actually plan a walk based on visiting several of the most special cloisters. Venice was home to many monasteries and convents, some of which are no longer there, but if you search you will still find cloisters.

My first memory of walking in a cloister wasn't in Venice but in Rome at the church of St Paul's Without the Walls. The memory is of a sunny March day, walking out of the church into the cloister and being assailed with the sudden smell of a boxwood hedge. The boxwoods were releasing the oil from their leaves in the noonday sunshine.

Sadly boxwood trees in Europe are now under threat from a disease called 'Box Blight'. It is so sad to see the brown leaves as the disease starts to 'lay claim' to a plant. Boxwood is the herb/tree traditionally used as a border in many herb gardens and links back to the distant Medieval past. Let's hope the blight passes or a cure is found soon.

Pulling this itinerary of cloisters together shows that although you can find cloisters throughout the city there is a very definite cluster around Castello. From Castello there is easy access by Vaporetto to San Giorgio Island. Some of the suggested cloisters are in Chorus Churches which you can visit with the pass or for three euros. Some are free and none is going to charge an exorbitant fee.

In the cloisters there may be tranquil cypress trees or the scent of orange blossom. If there was to be a setting for meditational thinking then it would be a cloister.

San Francesco Della Vigna
This church is a rare space in a busy city with a connected pair of lovely cloisters. These cloisters which are among the very oldest in Venice. There are cypress and orange trees and so you may hear birdsong in the cloister. A third larger cloister with only two Loggias is

only occasionally open to visitors. The arched loggia looks out onto a statue, lawns in the shape of a traditional herb bed and several green shrubs.

This church is built in the place where tradition says Saint Mark was driven ashore by a storm on his way back from Aquileia. Here he was told by an angel that the Lagoon was to be his resting place and that *'the city that shall rise on these lagoons will call you its protector'.* It was built on the site of a vineyard - hence the name. It is on the very edge of the city and can be empty even at the height of the season. Silence is still observed here.

The architecture and artwork are compelling with artists like Veronese and the Chorus website can give you those details. This is a focus on the Cloisters and the Churches of Venice. It is interesting architecturally as it has a renaissance interior by Sansovino and an exterior by Palladio. The rivals in architectural style combined together in this building.

Sant Elena

This is my favourite cloister. It was pretty much rebuilt in the early part of the twentieth century. During the Napoleonic occupation its art treasures were stripped out and its relics sent to San Pietro. It seems to have become a storage area and fell into ruin before the restoration.

It only has one cloister remaining but this has been cared for and renovated in recent years. It has a green central lawn and Roman style pillars holding up the arches. There are pots of plants around the wall of the loggia and ancient cobbles. It really is a place of peace to wander through in a quieter part of Venice.

San Pietro di Castello

This cloister might be called 'a cloister of faded grandeur'. Originally it was on a larger scale than other cloisters as it joined what was the main cathedral of Venice. San Pietro cloister now has a 'neighbourhood feel' as first floor windows of houses looking out onto the cloister. There is a shabby chic atmosphere with grass and plants growing up between cracks in the central courtyard but somehow this gives the place a special character.

If you are lucky then you may find a bench free to sit and watch the Venetian world go by. There is a grassed area outside the front of the church. We spent a lovely half hour here one summer. We sat on bench on the rather ragged grass. We people watched. We dog watched.

This church is worth seeking out. It was the original main Basilica until 1807. San Marco was then the Doge's chapel and San Pietro was much more the 'peoples church'.

The Basilica of San Pietro is located on the ancient island of Olivolo and in early Venice and before Sant Elena was developed it was almost at the edge of the lagoon. It is firmly rooted in its neighbourhood and is called San Pietro Di Castello. In the first settlement people started to build churches as soon as they began to feel safe and there has been a church on this site since 650. The remains of San Lorenzo Giustiniani the first patriarch of Venice are in an urn supported by angels high above the altar.

Over time various versions of the church were destroyed, re-built or re-modelled. In the 1500s Palladio designed a new facade which was significantly adapted by Smeraldi who was one of his students. I expected a medieval design the first time I visited San Pietro. I'd heard it was the first Basilica and made assumptions it would be similar to the Basilica on Torcello. However that early version of the cathedral has long since been destroyed by fire.

San Pietro has a spacious, roomy and uncluttered interior. The light shines in and the interior is very calm, mostly cream with some features highlighted with an unusual grey-green alabaster colour. The central dome brings in more light. Once I'd realised I was not in a dark, medieval, 'mosaiced' interior I adjusted and found it quite delightful.

Sant'Apollonia
This is in San Marco but very close to Castello. The romanesque cloister is special for creating an atmosphere of beauty and peacefulness. It seems more 'closed in' and austere than other cloisters. However there is a warmth in the brickwork and the loggias are impressive to walk through.

One website points out that in one corner of the cloister are modern stairs whose style seems at odds with the cloister. However, those stairs do in fact lead to modern and clean toilet facilities.

Originally the Benedictine Monastery of Sant'Appollonia it was built between the 12th and 13th centuries. In 1473 it became home to the clergy of the Cappella Ducale of Saint Mark's Cathedral. Now it houses the Diocesan Museum of Sacred Art and the Patriarchal Historical Archives.

The cloister could almost be a Roman building. The loggia /portico is a row of double arched lintels. A 13th century well with unusual rounded corners is located in the centre of the cloister.

La Pietà

This is a good place to end or stand your walk. It has no cloister but does have an amazing view. La Pietà is Vivaldi's church but on this walk today it is the setting with the Bacino as its backdrop and the Riva as its cloister which makes this a place to pause and reflect. From here you need to walk up the Riva degli Schiavonni to San Zaccaria or even a little futher to the Arsenale stop and take a vaporetto over to San Georgio.

San Giorgo Maggiore - Palladio

This is a world famous beautiful church which is quite different from the central island churches as it is very plain with just a few highlighted paintings.

There is a lovely cafe with superb views across to St Mark's. Climb the campanile for stunning views across the whole lagoon to Murano and beyond. There is more on the island later in the book.

The cloisters on San Giorgio are very different in style and are Palladio's cloisters. He designed the church and cloisters. Apparently you need to book in advance if you want to visit these cloisters but they are beautiful and it is worth the journey.

Madonna Dell Orto

This is in Cannaregio, so further from Castello. This church has a significantly sized cloister with no grass but ancient faded brickwork with a well and a tree in the centre. If you are staying in this area then you could start your 'journey through the cloisters' here and then walk on to Castello.

Santo Stefano

This is the same and if you are staying near La Fenice or on Dorsoduro you could start your walk here at the Santo Stefano cloisters. I nearly missed this one when I visited Santo Stefano. The cloisters have survived with a central grassy area and stone well.

San Lazzaro degli Armeni

If you have a longer stay in Venice then consider an afternoon visit to the island of San Lazzaro. In the mists of time this was a leper colony which gradually ceased being used and became uninhabited. In 1717 the Pope asked the Republic to give a group of Armenian monks a safe haven from the turmoil they have been facing in their own country. The gift was this small island of San Lazzaro. The monks worked to reclaim more of the marshland from the lagoon and the island has quadrupled in size since 1717.

It is possible to visit this small island at specific times. Just one guided tour takes place daily at 3.25 pm. and no reservation is needed. A monk or member of the wider Armenian community gives a guided tour in Armenian, Italian or English. A small donation is requested. The number 20 leaves from San Zaccaria at 15.10 hrs with a return at 17.25 hrs. There is a notice at the boat station with further information.

This place is a focus for Armenian culture. The Armenians have been persecuted over the centuries most significantly in the days of the Ottoman Empire. In the monastery there are rooms of ancient artefacts and a library of 200,000 historical books and ancient manuscripts. The first Armenian dictionary was developed here.

Lord Byron spent time on the island and became known as 'a friend of the Armenian people'. There is a plaque to remember him just outside the monastery. Byron apparently used to swim over from his residence on the Grand Canal. He taught himself Armenian and became skilled at translating books and contributing to the dictionary and grammatical reference book.

The vestibule to the library has a ceiling painted by Tiepolo. There is an individual collection of antiquities with Roman pottery, glass and an Egyptian mummy.

Napoleon disbanded the monasteries, removing some artwork and melting down the bells. San Lazzaro was somehow left in peace. The monastery church with its stained glass windows and campanile with its eastern cupola are impressive. The campanili is a familiar landmark on the vaporetto ride over to the Lido.

However it is the cloister which is the focus here. It is beautiful haven of serenity. It is a large cloister and still functions as a cloister for the monks who live on the island. In the cloister there are some archaeological finds and a well which pre-dates the monastery. The cloister gardens are lovely. Apparently there used to be a small flock of sheep to keep the lawns trimmed.

Momento di Mindfulness
Calm Contemplative Cloister

A cloister is designed to be a reflective space. Seeking out these calm cloisters and walking through the covered loggias and arches is an original contemplative moment.

However you can enhance this reflective experience with a multi-sensory mindful meditational approach.

Multi-Sensory Thinking:
- Gaze and notice the covered walkway around the cloister. Look up at the ceiling and down at the paving stones. Look out to the centre of the cloister and the well in the centre. Notice the grass, flowers or faded brickwork.
- Take out a tissue with a drop of an essential oil like lavender, frankincense, cypress, geranium or clary sage. Breathe and absorb the scent.
- Imagine hearing plainsong chanting (sometimes called Gregorian chant). Listen for any birdsong or voices.
- Focus on your footsteps and the feel of the marble or stone as you walk slowly around the cloister.
- Touch the marble and stonework and feel the relative warmth or coolness to touch.

Find that still small centre of contentment & serenity; that still small place of calm.

You could almost stretch out time while walking in a cloister.

Mid-Morning in Campo San Barnaba

This is a small campo chosen to showcase how each campo can give you a wide range of mindful opportunities. Finding your own favourite campo will depend where you are staying. San Barnaba is in Dorsoduro and close to San Polo and Santa Margherita. It isn't far from the furthest side of San Marco or the boat ride over from Giudecca. It is furthest from Cannaregio.

This book covers the largest campos - Santa Margherita, San Polo, San Stefano, San Giovanni et Paulo, Santa Maria Formosa and Il Ghetto. There are many smaller but still significant campo like San Barnaba. Sometimes it is the unexpected 'find' which becomes precious.

One day while wandering a different way to the direction the yellow signs suggested, between Rialto and Accademia, we discovered a small rectangular calle with a lovely stone well, water fountain and a florist. The florist was using the water fountain for the flowers and so this 'calle' felt like a creative space. I've looked on the map of San Polo and there are three florists on it and I've no idea which one we stumbled across that day. It doesn't matter. Mindful Venice is all about coming across places which you notice and make you think a little differently. Everyone will find their own places during a walk through the calles of Venice. So let's give some focus to Campo San Barnaba.

You are on a film set. If you have ever seen the film 'Indiana Jones and the Last Crusade' then you will recognise the facade of this church in San Barnaba. This is the place where Indiana discovers the hidden crypt and tunnel. It is also the place where he emerges from the fiery tunnel startling some tourists having coffee at a bar.

The building is no longer a church and holds an interactive exhibition of the machines of Leonardo Da Vinci. The church has been re-modelled over time but the campanile which is a thousand years old is one of the oldest in Venice. In the film Summertime this campo is where Katherine Hepburn fell into the canal - so watch your step!

You can browse the shelves of a delicatessen - a specialist cheese and wine shop. The Enogastronomia Pantagruelica has wines, salami and cheese. It is more than a delicatessen as it is possible to buy and eat a simple yet delicious meal of cheese, meats and olives here. The store also has a special regional Amarone. Amarone is a warm, full flavoured wine with low acidic levels, often aged up to five years. It has a 15% alcoholic proof level so seems fortified. It is something to drink as a liqueur after a meal - my partner will choose Grappa but I would always choose Amarone when offered.

Turn around and you will see Grom. Grom is one of the best Gelateria in the city. Real flavour and worth stopping. The newer flavours seem to be especially individual. I've just looked and in February their special flavour was ricotta (from sheep's milk) and fig ice cream.

Just outside the campo is one of the sites of Venice which always makes me feel 'glad hearted' as it embodies a sense of Venetian community. You will find two boats on the canal at the edge of Campo San Barnaba which are in fact a market stall outside a small greengrocers.

These boat stalls are an array of fruit and vegetables. Here you will find produce for every day cooking. The stalls are always busy in the morning. This is the essence of the neighbourhood. It seems the stall has been here for at least 70 years. You will find it open every day except Sunday. You need to visit in the morning as it will be closed by lunchtime. Look out for the large tub of prepared artichokes at the edge of the boat. This may be one stall but it is almost a market in itself, filled with the life and character of the locality.

If you do visit Campo San Barnaba then it's not far to visit the larger and vibrant Campo Margherita.

Momento di Mindfulness
Small Corner of Venice

Choose something to eat from one of the shops mentioned above. A gelato, some olives and cheese or some fruit from the boat stall. When you eat then make sure you eat mindfully. Remember the raisin mindfulness exercise where every mouth movement and taste is considered carefully 'in real time' and becomes a mindful meditation.

Make your whole visit to this or a different small campo into a focused, multi-sensory experience. As you explore make mental notes of the multi-sensory aspects. The shade or sunshine, the heat or chilly weather, the smell of coffee, the taste of the ice cream, the sight of San Barnaba Campanile and the market boats.

Take photos to remind and remember your visit to a small corner of Venice.

Call at Ca'Rezzonico

Many years ago, in 1986, my partner and I went to Venice on a rainy day. It was his first visit to Venice. We had travelled on an overnight bus from the UK to stay at a resort near Venice. It rained and rained and this was unusual weather for late May. I wanted to see Robert Browning's house so we made our way out of Piazza San Marco towards the Accademia Bridge and got lost in Dorsuduro until we finally found Ca'Rezzonico.

The beauty of it was that Ca'Rezzonico wasn't fully restored but somehow seemed more authentic because of it. It felt as though we were exploring a real Venetian house. Since then Ca'Rezzonico has been renovated by the city and is now an impressive museum and gallery. Occasionally as I walk around the beautifully updated rooms I feel a little wistful for the shabbier Palazzo we finally discovered after getting lost on that rainy May day.

If you have an enthusiasm for art then you need to visit the Accademia, the Palazzo del Seminario with their timeless collections or the Guggenheim collection with its modern art and special sculpture gardens with a view of the Grand canal.

However you may prefer to choose a smaller museum for your mindful artistic Venetian moments. If you are looking for a smaller, more individual art gallery then Ca'Rezzonico may well be just the place. It is one of the later Palazzos and focuses on *Settecento Veneziano*. The art gallery showcases Venetian paintings including Guardi and Tiepolo. On the second floor rooms are set up to depict this period with a lady's bedroom and dressing room.

In the 1880s, it became the home of Robert Browning who died of bronchitis here in 1889. The American portrait painter John Singer Sargent also had a studio in Ca'Rezzonico Palazzo.

There is a garden with a loggia with wisteria and a traditional knot pattern design. There are lovely views of the Grand Canal from the windows. When you tire there is a tea room.

Ca' Fujiyama, Tea Room Beatrice

One hot August day we came across this special place. In Calle Lunga near San Barnaba. This is where I discovered Oolong Tea. More specifically Ty Guan Yin tea or Tung Ting tea. I started on a journey of discovery finding refreshing weaker tea in this tea garden on a hot summer's day.

I love tea but I tend towards the very strong malty Assam rather than the less vibrant Darjeeling. Oolong was different, being clear and refreshing with no need for milk or lemon. The small Oriental Teapot with extra water made Oolong a very long drink. My partner had the smoky Pu-Ehr and it wasn't for me. Oolong was perfect. I bought a packet and made it last until my next visit to Venice.

The Tearooms have some tables and a display of tea and cakes inside - so it's very much an all-weather place. There is an attractive courtyard garden outside. with large leafy green plants, jasmine and wisteria.

We went back the next year and my partner had the Matcha (green tea) Cappuccino. It was a unique experience and you can search online and find images of this very individual cappuccino. I stayed true to my Oolong and didn't regret it.

Momento di Mindfulness
'Secret Garden Inside'

Just make the moments here last. Take your time choosing and ordering your type of tea or coffee. There are also cakes and traditional pastries.

Maybe make this a 'cappo and biscuit' or a 'tea and cake' moment.

Whatever you do keep focused and take it slowly and notice the details around you.

If it is summer then spend time in the tea garden and focus on the green foliage and the courtyard walls which give this 'secret garden' some shelter.

'Mist Muffled' Bells

Morris talks of the 'mist muffled' bells of December. The bells of San Trovarso Church, a church I know from attending its Advent Concerts are pointed out as having a different type of peel and 'resembling alpine cow bells'.

Across Venice there are times when the city resonates and echoes with the sounds of bells chiming. The difference in timing means the bells don't ring at the same time and the bells last longer until the last bell fades away. Bells are part of the essential soundscape of Venice.

Bells chime,

Time tolls,

Sounding hours,

Seasonal Sounds

Ringing in Christmas

Chiming for Easter

Momento di Mindfulness
Making a Sensory Memory - Oil infused travels

Anchor another memory or two by making a sensory connection. Take a hankie (handkerchief) and put a drop or two of essential oil on it. Smell the fragrance. I usually choose Clary Sage or Geranium but it can be whatever you prefer. When you sit at a bar or return to your hotel take out the hankie and inhale the fragrance while you remember your walk.

Oil infused travels must surely be stronger if the olfactory parts of the brain are involved in creating the memory. I always carry a hankie with essential oil on it when travelling so I can keep calm if faced with an unexpected delay or turbulence on an aircraft.

If you don't have a cotton handkerchief then Venice is actually a good place to invest in one - whether from a souvenir shop or one of the linen shops in Venice or Burano. Of course a paper tissue, the inevitable Kleenex will do just as well.

Part 5

LATE MORNING

"And now come with me, for I have kept you too long from your gondola: come with me, on an autumnal morning, to a low wharf or quay at the extremity of a canal, with long steps on each side down to the water"

John Ruskin, The Stones of Venice

Timeless Traghetto

Traghetto means ferry. The boats are large gondola-style boats without decorations on their bows or brocade covered chairs. They are rowed by two oarsmen; one stands behind the passengers like a traditional gondolier, the other closer to the bow.

Traghetti take pedestrians across the Grand Canal at a few designated places. They are designed for locals to travel quickly across the canal; perhaps to reach the nearest supermarket. The crossing takes about five minutes.

In the past, until 1854, there was only one bridge across the Grand Canal. Today there are four bridges. There is also the Number 1 Vaporetto which darts from one bank of the canal to the other. Yet this traditional form of transport can still be found. Crossing the Grand Canal by traditional traghetto may be the nearest to a Gondola ride many of us will ever have.

There used to be thirty routes but now there are only seven. The two often most likely to be open are:

- Rialto Fish Market to Ca' Doro

- San Toma to Sant Angelo

Traghetto crossings are shown on some Venice street maps (look for straight lines across the Grand Canal). You'll often see signs on buildings pointing towards a traghetti station.

It is traditional to stand but you are free to sit. The locals will have had years of practice at standing up for the crossing. Hand your money to the oarsman as you join or leave and you really need to have the exact money ready.

The crossing opening times are unpredictable, but that's part of the experience. I admit to having no idea of the timetables or when the decision is made for a particular route to be open.

If you arrive at a ferry point and the crossing is closed then practice 'acceptance' and take a breath and find the Number 1 vaporetto or cross by a bridge. Go back later or another day. You may find it open the next time.

I would find it difficult to be mindful during a traghetto crossing, due to trying to keep my balance and take in the scenery of the canal. However watching the traghetto go back and forward has potential for a mindful and focused 5 minutes out of your itinerary.

Momento di Mindfulness
Compass as a Guide

Imagine a compass resting in the palm of your hand. It gives a sense of direction. A compass together with a map helps us find our way whether on isolated moorland or desert landscape. Apps for maps on mobile phones now give us step by step directions on journeys.

Yet the compass has been a tool used for centuries to guide people and ships home to port.

If you have no compass then look at the map of Venice and choose a direction – north, south, east west and walk that way. You will find something interesting whichever direction you take.

If you want to download a compass app onto your cell phone and choose a direction and walk that way. The compass will keep you focused on a specific direction. Just don't follow it so rigorously you fall into a canal!

The metaphor of a compass has been used for life, think of the phrase 'a moral compass'. When we have to make decisions the guide of our inner compass based on our inner values and preferences helps us find the way through.

Frari & Farmacia - Campo San Polo

It was in Campo San Polo in late December 2018 that I decided to write this book. It was a sunny winters day and the features of the campo stood out in the sunshine and shadows. It was late morning, so the ice rink wasn't open yet, but people were stopping to talk and shopping for Christmas. There were empty benches free to sit and watch the world go by. I could gaze at the ancient buildings in this wide irregular square.

Later in the day as we returned through the campo children were out playing or skating on the ice rink. Lots of small dogs were 'talking the air'. My mindful Venice project started here. The other campos are equally special; but I know this one best as it is closest to the hotel where we've stayed in recent years.

Several years ago I discovered the Farmacia & Erobistica (Herbal Pharmacy) of Dr Buratti. This is now run by his children and has the most amazing essential oils. I called to buy pino (pine) for Christmas and my favourite geranium oil.

This Farmacia/Erboristica is one of the oldest in the city. It is famous for the preparation of essential oils and herbal tisanes. There is also a range of supplements and natural beauty products. Inside the furnishings give a historical feeling of a pharmacy from a hundred years ago. Vases and containers are displayed which would have held the products in the past along with terracotta statues of Galen and Aesculapius.

 Momento di Mindfulness
Contemplative Campo … Pause at San Polo

There are usually benches free to sit on and rest and watch campo life pass by. Gaze at the campo and the warm greetings and interactions of the local people.

Maybe go into Dr Buratti's pharmacy and buy some lavender or geranium oil. Put some on a handkerchief and inhale the soothing smell. Stay quiet and contemplative in a corner of the campo.

Campo San Polo is the largest campo in Venice, only Piazza San Marco is larger. The route from the Rialto Bridge to the Accademia Bridge passes through Campo San Polo and the Frari church. Around the area are narrow calles with some interesting, individual shops on either side. The small shops sell artisanal jewellery, stationery, gloves, clothes with some interesting souvenirs. A shop selling candle holders reflecting light from a small tealight caught my eye and I secured a true bargain. A few years ago I discovered Castiglia Boutique at the foot of Ponte San Polo with a collection of elegant yet comfortable clothes with specialist crafted fabrics and my own 'collection' of 'souvenirs' has grown over time. Of course these individual local shops are interspersed with the more usual souvenir shops so you need to look carefully.

In the early days of the Republic this area was agricultural with animals grazing here. In 1493 it was paved over with a water catching well in the centre. It was a lively place with bullfights, masked balls and political speeches. In 1548 Lorenzino de Medici was assassinated in the campo by two hired killers.

It is still a gathering place for Feste and Carnival activities. In the summer movies are screened in the open air and this 'movie theatre' continues into the September Film Festival. In the winter there is an ice rink and stalls with hot wine.

In the far corner is a Palazzo housing the Guardia di Finanza Regional Command Centre. At Christmas there was a display of small miniature models of Christmas scenes. We wandered into a free exhibition in an impressive palazzo. It is always worth looking out for this type of small, free exhibition as it gives access to medieval buildings you would otherwise never see. The Frari and San Polo Churches are close by.

San Polo is the local church, often closed for services, which shows it's importance to the neighbourhood. The Church has a treasury of artwork. The art somehow stands out more here than at some other churches, perhaps due to the austere brickwork interior. Look for Tintoretto's 'The Last Supper' and 'The Assumption of the Virgin with Saints'. At the main altar is Veronese's 'The Marriage of the Virgin' and at the other altar in the left aisle is Tiepolo's 'The Virgin appearing to San Giovanni Nepomuk'. As with any Chorus church the other artwork and detailed information about architectural features can be found on the visitors sheet given on entry to the church or online.

The Frari is special place. More grandly called Santa Maria Gloriosa dei Frari it began to be built in 1231. This was at the beginning of the fervour surrounding St Francis and the Franciscan order. The Doge donated land for a monastery and church for the Franciscans. The original church was too small so a three nave church was planned to replace it. Having seen a replica of St Francis original hut and church in Assisi you can see the grandeur must have taken over the Franciscan order at this point in its history. The Frari was completed in 1338 with the campanile following in 1396.

It is a place to wander and where you will always find something you have never noticed before. There are side chapels to explore. There are corners where you feel as though you are the first person to discover them that day. It is certainly a church of artists. Titian is buried here. The Frari is a treasury of artwork and sculptures and again the information sheet given when you go into the church is a good guide.

The Chorus website sums up the Frari by saying 'over the centuries the Basilica has become a veritable treasure-chest of exceptional works of art'. Titian's 'The Assumption' and 'Virgin Mary from Cà Pesaro' are famous artworks. Bellini's triptych of the Virgin Mary and Saints is a well-known masterpiece.

In the chapel of the Fiorentini is a wooden sculpture of John the Baptist by Donatello. Every side chapel has art to catch the eye. Even the choirstalls are ornately carved. The Chorus information says the Cloister of St Anthony is usually closed to public admittance but we've certainly been in it more than once. It's a quiet and inspirational place to wander into if you do find it open.

Momento di Mindfulness
Cloak of Serenity meditation

In silence listening for that still small voice of calm.
It's a central focus of mindful thinking
Imagine serenity.
And how serenity feels
A cloak of serenity

Wintery Warm Light
Imagine streams of wintery warm light reaching you. The warm light gently touching your body. If you are out and about then imagine your hands warming, your toes tingling with the light and warm rising up your body. Warm, wintery white light giving you a relaxed feeling of serenity.

If you are able to sit or lie down somewhere quietly then this exercise can be given more focus and carried out like a variation of a body scan meditation. In the same way as you would for a body scan meditation consider each part of the body in sequence. Your attention focused on your body and becoming relaxed. This time the difference is that you imagine the warm glowing light, sometimes called a 'point of light" touching your fingers, hand, arm, elbow and so on.

The more structured meditational exercises like 'body scan' or 'point of light' are practiced the more connections in the mind strengthen. Research is showing that the connections, or 'the firing and wiring' in the brain's processing centres changes and stress responses seem to be more resilient.

The warm wintery white light giving you a cloak of serenity. If it helps imagine this cloak as a costume for the Venetian Carnivale – a long, flowing winter white cloak giving a feeling of confident serenity.

Summery Balm of Cool Air
As I write this I realise my own vacations in La Serenissima in the last three years have been in the winter. If you are visiting in a hot, heat wave then you would need to change the warm, wintery light to a balm of coolness. The point of light can be a cool (or icy) sensation as and when you prefer. Imagining cool air touching and melting and moving through your body.

Casa di Goldoni

This Palazzo close to Campo San Polo was the home of the Venetian playwright Goldoni. Built in the 15th century it feels even older as it is built in the style of the early Venetian palazzos. As you walk past Casa di Goldoni then you glimpse an inner courtyard with a stone well and an open staircase supported by what resembles Gothic arches. Terracotta flooring, an ancient water gate and lovely leaded arched windows.

And of course Commissario Guido Brunetti of the Donna Leon novels lives only a few minutes away from Campo San Polo.

 *Momento di Mindfulness*
(S)Pace to Think

Walk with pace. Notice how your pace varies as you spend the morning walking through the labyrinth of calles. Towards the end of your walk start to consciously slow your pace. Instead of a Race Slow Down the Pace.

Breathe in rhythm to match your walking pace. Slow your rate of breathing. As you walk with a slower pace your thoughts will slow down too. Start to think in a focused multi-sensory way.

Notice what you see and hear around you. Feel the temperature of the air around you. Notice the scent of the sea air. Sea air is different. Sea air feels invigorating. Whether it is negative ions, air humidity or a taste of sea salt ... who knows. It just feels energising and reviving.

Breathing establishes harmony. Feel the connection with breathing and walking pace. Start to focus on the buildings around you. Walk along calles which connect you to the past. Connect to history.

There will be times during your holiday when you walk slowly and consciously. Guido Brunetti has a game he plays every day of finding something new to appreciate. Look out for something every day to be added to your special memory bank.

Momento di Mindfulness
No destination in mind

Make your starting point somewhere a little different. Maybe the Giudecca Island, the Cannaregio Canal, Campo Santa Margherita or the streets near La Fenice. Wander with no destination in mind. You will probably wander into the network of quieter canals. Last time we got lost was in the busiest San Marco Sestiere somewhere between La Fenice and Santo Stefano. We found new places and were surprised to find we were a little lost. If you do realise you are lost then Venice is a small city and you will soon find your way back to a signpost. But take the opportunity to find a moment of thoughtful reflection. Stand still for a second and find that inner core of stillness. You may be temporarily 'off grid' but you are firmly grounded and 'at home with yourself'

Veneziano – Community of Castello
Veneziano is the unique dialect of Venice. With a different intonation pattern and consonants it resembles languages from further east towards Byzantium. In actuality it sounds more like a separate language than a dialect. In the Donna Leon novels some of the characters only really speak the local Veneziano. Guido Brunetti moves into dialect when he hopes to establish shared close communication with someone. It forms a link straight away. Venetians recognising Venetians. Most often this is when the story is set in the community of Castello, where Brunetti lived and went to school and learned Veneziano.

Part 6

NOON/ MID-DAY

"Venice… A splendour of miscellaneous spirits."

John Ruskin

Passeggiare sulle Fondamenta

Fondamenta is a word you will hear often in Venice. A Fondamenta is a pathway with mooring running alongside a canal. Fondamenta is the word used, except when the pathway is next to the Grand Canal or the lagoon edge when it would be called a Riva.

Fondamenta means 'foundation' or base. They are great places to take a walk, looking around you and noticing things like the different shades of the water or the colours of the buildings.

The main Fondamenta are:

Misericordia
Cannaregio
Nuove
Zattere
Arsenale

And many more ... notice the signs and collect some Fondamenta!

 *Momento di Mindfulness*
Dawdling Days

This is such a lovely old fashioned word and concept. The verb 'to dawdle'. Slow travel in practice. Take time today to 'dawdle' along a Fondamenta noticing the scenery around you.

Venice is a seasonal city. Migrating swallows and house martins arriving and departing. Geese moving with the change in weather and season. The hot dusty streets of high summer and the opaque mists of winter.

More than this though it is a city which can change from hour to hour depending on the weather. The sun really does illuminate the colours. The city on a cloudy or misty day is still beautiful but the colours which stand out seem different. On a sunny day it is the yellow, golden ochre, terracotta whereas on a misty day it is the cream, grey, blues.

104

Mist and Soft Focus Maybe you notice a shaft of light from a doorway permeating through the fog. Glowing warm light through windows dissolving the mist.

Sunshine on water. Silvery sparkles making a trail on the water. Yellows and orange colours standing out on the buildings.

Campo dei Ghetto

Campo dei Ghetto Nuovo is a quiet place to pause and reflect. It is enclosed by historical palazzos. Some of these palazzos are the tallest buildings in Venice. The area needed to expand was restricted and so with ingenuity the buildings grew taller and taller. There are benches and some trees for shade and depending on the time of year a couple of cafes should be open. Campo dei Ghetto is a good place to sit in a cafe and watch the world go by.

Of course you will notice the armed guard keeping watch from the booth at one end of the campo. This is the middle of the Venetian Ghetto and there is constant vigilance nowadays. The word Ghetto is chilling because of recent 20th century history and the shadow of Warsaw and other ghetto during the Holocaust. Many Venetian Jews escaped before the Nazi occupation but 246 remained. In 1943 and 1944 those people were taken and sent to Auschwitz or a concentration camp near Trieste. Only eight returned to Venice. A bronze memorial giving the names and ages of the victims can be found on two walls in the campo.

From 1516 Jewish moneylenders, doctors and merchants were allowed to leave the Ghetto and go about their business during the day. However at night, and during Christian holidays, the community was locked up on the island of the Ghetto Nuovo. 'Geto' comes from the word 'foundry' and this was originally the island of the new foundry. The heavy gates were locked allowing no one to leave or enter. Napoleon abolished this in 1797 but it had continued for centuries.

There are some very individual bakers close to the campo and it is well worth stopping to buy pastries. Along the edge of the Ghetto on the Cannaregio Canal there is a kosher restaurant called Gam Gam. An assortment of Mezza, including falafels, served with homemade lemonade with a mint leaf is a real pleasure. You sit outside next to the canal looking towards the Guglie Bridge. We've had several three course meals here to celebrate birthdays, but the simple Mezza are my firm favourite. Last time we ate at Gam Gams I returned home and bought some little china dishes, inspired to begin cooking Mezza at home. The crisp aubergine dishes are particularly delicious.

In the campo there is a museum of Jewish life and three historical synagogues can be visited as part of a tour from the museum. The synagogues are world famous, built into the upper stories of houses. With designs by Venetian architects there is a very 'Venetian Baroque' style to these synagogues. Magnificent chandeliers and balconies give the feel of a theatre as much as a religious building.

The campo is busy with galleries, glass shops, books and bakeries. Venetian Jews return here for religious services in those synagogues which are still used. There is a yeshiva for study. The Ghetto is a definite centre of community.

It is possible to walk to the ghetto from the lagoon side and walk back on the Via Nova along the canal. Today the Ghetto feels a vibrant and positive place.

Momento di Mindfulness
Loss, Grief and Hope

Close your eyes and imagine a busy scene in the campo. Children playing. Seniors talking and sharing memories. It's busy and lots is happening. The sun shining and you sense a general feeling of contentment with life.

Open your eyes and close them again. This time imagine only about 8 people in the campo. Behind the 2 or 3 people are a host of shadow shapes of 200 lost Jewish people including children and elderly people. This time a contrasting sense of loss with intense grief.

Open your eyes and look at today and the scene around you. There will be people going about their business. People sitting at cafes drinking a cappuccino. A pleasant scene of daily life in a campo. Feel gratitude for the day and its serenity.

Back to Scuole?
It's taken me a long time to understand the system of Venetian Scuole. Both it's Scuole Grande and Scuole minor. Then I realised they were similar to what in the UK we call 'mutual' or 'friendly societies' providing support for members in times of need.

The Scuole in Venice weren't just for the nobles. Most Venetians belonged to a Scuole and they usually linked with an artisanal trade. The nearest English word is probably 'Guild'. These mutual societies gave aid to members in need. The sick or widowed benefitted. Over time each Scuole began to want to showcase its headquarters with impressive artwork and furnishings. There seems to have been a definite element of competition between Scuoles. The organisations began to build schools, hospitals, orphanages and workhouses for those who were destitute.

They became a source of sponsorship for artists and led to Venice becoming a hotbed of innovation in medieval art. The focus was on the stories of the lives and martyrdom of favourite saints. Often a Scuole would link with local churches and side chapels might be designed and funded by a Scuole.

In Napoleonic days they came under stricter central control. Napoleon seems to have liked uniformity and organisation of civic services. Many works of art and ancient documents were taken from the Scuole into government ownership.

Six Scuole Grande stood out as the most affluent and influential in the Republic but there is documentation for over nine hundred Scuole Piccolo. The Scuola Grande di San Rocco has an upper hall with wondrous frescos by Tintoretto. There are Old Testament paintings on the walls and New Testament on the ceiling. The Scuola di San Giorgio degli Schiavoni has very individual art work by Carpaccio. It's suggested visitors take a mirror to view the painted ceiling in reflected glory. The buildings themselves are remarkable if you look beyond the paintings.

Mournful cherubs at Misericordia
The Scuola Grande della Misericordia in Cannaregio district is one of the major 'Scuole Grandi'.

The original plans for the Misericordia were drawn up by Sansovino. The vast hall on the building's first floor remains one of the largest in the historical centre of Venice. These walls are decorated with frescoes in the style of Veronese.

The Misericordia has been restored. It is getting a reputation as a cultural centre, with events like seminars, conferences, performances and exhibitions.

Momento di Mindfulness
Viewpoints, Vistas and Horizons

Every holiday should have its own memory bank. Those visiting with an attentive, focused approach (sounds like mindfulness) will tend to bank sights, sounds into memory automatically.

Making the memories even stronger with mindfulness techniques makes sense. Try the ideas here as a way of adding strength and depth to memories so you can use the memories practically when you've returned home.

This is about finding your 'Viewpoints', your own special places to gaze out at the view of the city and lagoon.

Imagine that you have both narrow and wide view lens available. You are aiming for narrow focused and then wide panoramic camera shots.

Look at the view with a narrow lens focus. Notice the details in the buildings or on the boats.

Now change to a wide view lens and move your gaze out to the furthest and widest view you can see, If you want to change back to narrow lens again and contrast then do so.

While out walking look for Viewpoints with wide vistas: perhaps from a Fondamenta or a roof terrace. Look out taking in a wide, sweeping panoramic view of the city.

Also look for narrow focus Viewpoints: perhaps washing hanging out, an archway, a dark Sottoportego (covered alleyway)

Look for contrasting viewpoints: calles opening into wider campo spaces. See it differently. Make it different.

There is no reason why you shouldn't take photos to reinforce the memories. I find my visual memory is not as strong as my auditory memory and photos of places I stay does help me remember more when I'm home again.

When you return home then it may be a case of just closing your eyes and running through memories of holiday viewpoints. A short, focused meditational moment.

You can also integrate your memories into the final moments of a body scan meditation.

When you have run through the Body Scan then stay still and run the viewpoints in your mind. Remember the wide and narrow lens vistas.

Focus on a narrow lens view. Then widen it out to the full panoramic sweep.

Various Viewpoints, Vistas with the shimmering lagoon on the Horizon.

The Ferry to The Lido

The first time I ever saw Venice was from a ferry arriving from Punta Sabbioni. We arrived from a holiday at Lido de Jesolo on a day trip.

If you arrived in Venice by plane or train, bus or by ferry from Treporte to Fundamente Nuove then it is worth going out on a ferry just so that you get the spectacular view of the Doges Palace on the return trip.

The ferries leave from San Zaccaria. They stop at Lido and then on past the new sea defence barrier before they arrive at Punta Sabbioni. There are glimpses of the very edge of the lagoon where it merges with the Adriatic Sea. There is little to explore at Punta Sabbioni as it is pretty much a bus and ferry terminus. Often you can say to the ticket inspector that you are returning to Venice and just stay on the boat. Otherwise, depending on time of year you can get a coffee or drink in the bar at Punta Sabbioni before boarding the next boat back to Lido and Venice.

As the return ferry moves towards Lido you start to see your first glimpses of Venice in the far distance. Then as it moves away from Lido you can see Venice on the near horizon. The view you see will vary with time of year and time of day. There may be an early morning mist, a heat haze, a glorious blue sky or silvery grey clouds. There may be rain with the luminosity of the rain shining on the Istrian stone. It doesn't matter because it is still going to be special.

The ferry moves slowly past a couple of islands, getting closer and closer to Venice until you see San Marco, the Doge's palace and the Riva degli Schiavoni.

If it is a quieter time of year you will have an uninterrupted view. If it is the height of summer then other tourists will be jostling for position on the deck to get their snapshot of the scene. Take your photo. But ... look too, don't be so busy with your camera that you forget to actually look at the view.

This first view of Venice from the lagoon is a special moment in anyone's life. I still remember the excitement of my parents and grandmother when they first saw this view from the ferry in 1971. This is the same view the merchant adventurers would have seen when returning home to their city after a long voyage.

Slow Travel and Bird Spotting on the Lagoon

Slow travel on the Lagoon is gaining in popularity. It still isn't accessible yet for those on a budget. It would be lovely to take a trip on a sailing ship to San Francesco del Deserto but it is outside of most vacation budgets. Slow travel blogs now describe journeys out onto the lagoon in traditional bragozzo or fishing boats. It's possible to go out fishing for cuttlefish or looking for wild birds such as heron, sandpipers or avocets.

Even if you are unable to locate or afford a day in a traditional bragozzo by utilizing mindfulness strategies you are exploring the city and islands with consideration, focus and within the slow travel philosophy.

Momento di Mindfulness
Notice the 'Lagoon-scape'

When leaving Lido on a ferry keep gazing towards the scene you are approaching. While the city is still on the horizon then notice the details close by on the lagoon, even the ripples from the wash of a boat in front of the ferry.

Look out for seabirds, especially gulls, herons and egrets out on the lagoon in the distance. Gaze and give attention to the 'lagoon-scape'.

Momento Meditativo Multisensoriale
Contrasting Lagoon - Seasonal Seascape

Take the lagoon home with you. Make your own memory movie.

Imagine Venice from the air. Look for an aerial photo shot of Venice and the lagoon. Zoom in and enlarge the image. Focus on the shape and outline.

Close your eyes and imagine it in your mind.

Imagine the seasons and the changing scenery and seascape. See the green lugubrious reflective water of the hot summer and the grey, misty waters of winter. Imagine feeling the cold of the sleet and snow in the

Bora wind and the contrast of hot, dusty calles where you look for shade in the summer.

Harsh marshland giving shelter and becoming home to families. The lagoon barrier of the Lido protecting the city from the stormy seas of the Adriatic.

Go through you movie again with your eyes closed. Save your 'movie memory' and take it home with you to treasure.

Living the Lido in Changing Seasons
Much more so than on Venice island itself, the experience you have on the Lido will vary from season to season.

The journey across to Lido takes about ten minutes and you can take a vaporetto or one of the larger ACTV ferries. Sometimes in the early spring we have been almost the only passengers on a larger ferry. Occasionally in the summer we have been able to sit outside on a vaporetto as it makes its way over to Lido. Sitting outside right at the back of the boat on a summer's day is a lovely experience. Unless it is a foggy day you will get that spectacular view of San Marco from the Lido.

Spring: take the opportunity to walk down to the sea. The literal 'sea side' of the Lido. On a sunny spring day you will smell the sea, feel the breeze, those negative ions and ozone and be optimistic about the warmer summer days yet to come. The road leading down to the beach will have flowers and it is a gentle walk from the ferry down to the sea. Catch a glimpse of the open sea and enjoy that 'sea air'.

You can also walk along the lagoon side of the Lido. If you are staying in Venice a longer time then take the bus out towards Alberoni and the distant Palestrina. Palestrina is a fishing village at the far end of the Lido.

Summer: escape for a while from the hot dry streets of Venice and find the beach. There are ten kilometres of beach and it is the same long stretch of sand you would find at the holiday resort of Lido di Jesolo. Venice Lido is an attractive holiday resort with an art deco feel to it. You could spend time on the beach and hire an umbrella and lounger/deck chair or take a towel to the free beach.

 *Momento di Mindfulness*
Shells at the Seashore

You can walk and paddle along the sand for a very long way. Collect small shells and pebbles as you walk along the edge of the sea. There are small curly whirly, spiral and razor clam shells. The water is very calm and clean. Put an empty shell or two in your pocket or in your bag. You will come across this shell in the future at some point and it will remind you of your special walk on the beach.

Search out Malamocco, an unspoiled village that was once the home of the Doge and as important as Venice back in the early days of the Republic. Then the island thickens out again, with dune-backed beaches. Find your way out towards Alberoni and the quieter, wilder beaches of the Lido. The Lido sandbank has acted as a natural barrier protecting the lagoon and the city for centuries.

Autumn: if it is September then you will no doubt be 'celebrity spotting' at the Film Festival. If it is later in the season then cycling along the Lido becomes possible. The deciduous trees will be turning into vibrant Autumn colours before losing their leaves. You're more likely to have a misty day. This can be a good time of year to go to the local market. If you get on the vaporetto on Tuesday (market day) you will see local Venetians with their shopping trolleys ready to go 'a-marketing'.

You can find Pizzerias with wood fired ovens on Lido. Why not stop and have a leisurely pizza on the Lido.

Winter: the sky and sea seem to merge in shades of grey. Find a bar for hot chocolate. Cioccolata calda has a thick, almost pudding like texture in the cup. This hot chocolate is an experience in itself and where better than a cold winter's day on Lido.

The large ferries will give you a 'higher up' view and there are warm, inside areas - it may be too cold to sit outside.

Momento di Mindfulness
Press Pause

Sit on a bench and feel the sea breeze. Listen for the sound of bells in the distance. Gaze across the lagoon to the campanile in San Marco.

Smell the pine trees giving shade. Lido is filled with flowers and sometimes the scent of oleander drifts across.

Wondrous Window Boxes
There are parks and hidden gardens in Venice. There are more suggestions about secret gardens to visit in a later section.

However the city has a continuous colourful backdrop of window boxes. Look upwards from late spring to autumn (fall) and you will see an array of colour. Vibrant splashes of red, pinks, crimson, violet, white and yellow. The different shades of red geraniums blend together against the yellow, cream and terracotta of the buildings.

Geraniums (pelargoniums) in both the traditional and trailing varieties. Begonias are a plant I'd never choose for my own garden as I prefer the wilder herbs and flowers. However in Venice they seem a perfect plant. They thrive and give a wash of colour throughout the summer. The sea climate gives fewer frosts and they have a long season and may even overwinter. Together the geraniums and begonias are as much a part of Venice as the palazzos and canals.

In the winter you will see white and pink cyclamens, purple pansies with draping cascades of ivy, Winter flowering plants bravely giving colour during the cold, damp weather. Towards Christmas the window boxes may be sparkling with Christmas lights and their reflections in the glass of each window.

The window boxes may be terracotta, painted wood, usually framed by wrought iron curlicues. Together the container and its colourful cargo of flowers give pleasure to Venetians and visitors alike. They also create an ecosystem for insects like bees and ladybirds (ladybugs).

 Momento di Mindfulness
Strength & Vibrancy of Flowers

Consider the flowers growing in a small amount of soil in harsh salt filled air. The dry heat of summer, the torrential rains when the arid weather breaks towards the end of August. The gales and sleet of the winter. The plants face all elements as they look down on the city. Imagine the bees, caterpillars, butterflies, moths clustering close to the flowers in the summer. Each window box is its own miniature ecosystem.

Choose a window box today and focus on it for a minute. If it isn't too intrusive take a photo to remind you of tenacious strength in fragile conditions. When you are home and facing a difficult day remember the strength and vibrancy of a Venetian window box.

A Quiet Corner - Santa Maria dei Miracoli

In 1470s in Cannaregio an icon of the Madonna got quite a reputation for delivering miracles. People started to visit the scene which became even more famous when someone was resuscitated after being underwater for thirty minutes. Money was raised for a church to house the icon. The icon of the Madonna is still there and on display on the altar.

The church is interesting as it was built by a local craftsman who was experienced at making monuments in marble. It was built of brick then covered with a marble facade. It is a small church but has the illusion of being larger than it is due to the patterned marble and design of the windows. The marble and windows together give a light and airy atmosphere. It's an eye catching building. The marble gives a cool atmosphere on a hot summer's day

It began to be restored in 1987 because the marble slabs were at the point of being beyond repair. They were absorbing and accumulating salt from the lagoon so each slab was removed and treated to remove the salt. The restoration was expected to take two years and actually took ten.

This small Renaissance church is tucked away in a small calle next to a canal. It isn't too far from the Campo dei Ghetto and combines well with a visit there.

Momento di Mindfulness
Climate of Contrasts

The climate in Venice has greater contrast between Summer and Winter than most European cities. The dry, dusty heat of August and the misty murky days, with Acqua Alta high tides and risk of flooding in the Autumn and Winter.

Think of a climate of contrasts and opposites.
High and low tide; high and low temperatures.
Harshness and resilience in survival

Part 7

LUNCH – EARLY AFTERNOON

"If I were not King of France, I would choose to be a citizen of Venice".

Henry III

Via Giuseppe Garibaldi

Several years ago we spent a holiday in an apartment in Castello. It was a quiet apartment in a very narrow calle close to the Arsenale vaporetto stop. We lived side by side with locals. It was one of those places where you could almost see into the living room of the neighbour across the calle and vice versa.

It was a very short walk to the Riva degli Schiavoni and the vaporetto stop. If our footsteps turned in the other direction it was less then 5 minutes to the Arsenale gates. The stone lions guarding the entrance next to a bar and restaurant which served the most curious red wine which was slightly fizzy (sparkling) and refreshing.

On that holiday we discovered the Via Garibaldi. It's a wide, open and spacious street. It was where we came to shop for bread, cheese and other items in the small supermercato. Every morning we went early to Via Garibaldi to visit the shops and a couple of market stalls to buy food for breakfast.

This was a special place as it was clearly a community. It was clear that people had been to school together, knew each other's families. Venetians stopping to greet and chat together. Today there is still a wide range of shops, cafes, bars, greengrocers, laundry, shoe shop, ironmongers/hardware shop.

Children play out. Dogs go out for their walks. People stand talking in groups. Even in the winter they come out to be social and enjoy the late afternoon sunshine.

You might glance down a side alley and see the washing, high up, strung across the calle giving a colourful pattern from house to house. Look to the other side of the street and see the entrance to the Giardini Park with places to sit in the summer and some welcome shade. This is the quieter side of the Giardini, not the section with the Biennale Pavilions.

The time of day when this happens will vary according to the time of year, but there have been several times when we have been lucky enough to visit the Via just as the shade is retreating and the sun moving across to 'enlighten' the houses and cafes. On my last visit, during December, the sun started to warm the street at about lunchtime. It will vary season to season.

Now whenever I come to Venice, even if I stay way over in Dorsoduro, I always try to return to the Via. On my last visit I called in an ironmongers and found some large rush table mats. You will find pharmacy, shoe shop, toy shop and whatever you need on the Via Garibaldi. To walk up the street and absorb the atmosphere. To have a coffee and a pastry in a bar. It's a quietly inspiring place.

We know the Venetians are leaving Venice year on year as a result of property prices rocketing due to tourism. However in places like Via Garibaldi, Campo San Polo, Santa Maria Formosa I sense something of the sort of family values approach to life and living which my grandparents talked about. It's rare now to have extended families and feeling of community in the UK.

The Via isn't far from San Marco. If you walk up the Riva Degli Schiavoni you will find this place. If you come into Via Garibaldi from a side street as we did on our first visit and walk towards the end of the street you will start to glimpse the lagoon. You almost gasp as you walk out onto the Riva and catch sight of the Bacino with the view over towards San Giorgo. Last time I visited was on 23rd December and it was a bright sunny day. The mist was dispersing and the sunlight was glittering on the water.

At the other end of the Via you can see where the canals start and boats are stored. It feels abrupt and truncated and that's because it is! Via Garibaldi was originally a canal which was filled in by Napoleon. This wide street isn't a campo but it has the definite feel of a place which is the centre of a neighbourhood.

Momento di Mindfulness
The Warmth of the Sun

Notice the patterns of shade and sun on the Via Garibaldi. It can be shady but as the sun rises the shade gives way to the sun's warmth. Because it is a wide street this contrast between sun and shade is much more noticeable than in the narrow calles.

Next time you do a Body Scan meditation then spend a few moments afterwards visualising a street which is shady. There is a slight damp chill in the air. You notice a ray of sunshine striking the street. This gradually grows stronger and wider as it covers the street with light and warmth. Relax in the warmth of the imagined sunlight.

Tramezzini & Pasticceria

I first heard of tramezzini while reading Donna Leone's Commissario Guido Brunetti series of novels. The food of the Brunetti family is a vital aspect of the stories. Occasionally Brunetti cannot make it home for lunch. At these times Brunetti may call into a bar and take a glass of wine and some tramezzini. These sounded like plain white bread flat sandwiches. However one day I stopped to gaze at one of the most attractive window displays in Venice. The window was at Bar Alla Toletta, near the Toletta canal on the walk from Rialto to the Accademia.

The sandwiches are made differently to the flat English version. They are bursting with filling with a covering of thin white bread. These are a totally different type of sandwich. Fillings such as Parma or cooked ham, mozarella and mayonnaise, tuna and onion or artichoke, ricotta and spinach are available. Tremezzini are found throughout the city but the 'eye catching' window display at Bar Toletta is where I first noticed them. You will also find Panini, crostini baguettes and pizza squares. Enough to keep you going before an afternoon of sightseeing. Best to go at lunchtime or early afternoon when the tramezzini are fresh.

I've stayed close-by Bar Toletta and often call into the Pasticceria next door (also called Toletta) for a small cake - the ricotta or zabaglione filled cannoli being a favourite. The range is 'wondrous' and you can eat in or easily have several pastries put into a box to take away. An inexpensive way to find fuel for the miles of walking you are likely to be doing.

Momento di Mindfulness
Tasting Tramezzini

Purchase a savoury snack at Bar Toletta or a small bread bun or dry
cake at the Pasticceria next door. Of course any bakery or sandwich
shop would work fine for this exercise. Find a quiet place to eat your
snack. Eat mindfully in the same way as in the raisin exercise. Make
each movement a conscious movement. Breaking off a piece of the
bread or cake, taking it to your mouth, tongue, teeth and lips moving to
make the bread into a small ball shape to swallow. The swallow being
triggered and starting again with the next piece of bread.

Antica Locanda Montin
Ruskin stayed at The Danielle, but he also frequented some smaller
establishments on the other side of the city. La Calcina with a view out
over the Giudecca Canal on the Zattere was the hotel where he wrote
most of 'The Stones of Venice'. It is still possible to eat, and even stay
in, some of Ruskin's special places in Venice.

Back in Dorsoduro is the Antica Locanda Montin which was one of
Ruskin's favourite haunts. The walls have wood panelling with
numerous paintings from local artists and guests. Some of the paintings
are good, some are mediocre but they are all cherished. The Locanda
has rooms to let and a pergola-covered back garden where the tables
are set for al fresco breakfast and dining in summer. Ruskin loved
sitting here.

We ate Christmas Dinner here in 2018 and loved the Antica, ironically
without knowing about its historical connection with Ruskin

Keeping up with the Contarinis
Scala Contarini Del Bovolo
This open spiral staircase on the outside of the Contarini palazzo is
unique. It's down a narrow calle close to Campo Manin, midway
between Campo San Bartolo at Rialto and Campo Santo Stefano.
It is inspired by Byzantine architecture with an almost frivolous, frothy
Baroque look with its high arches and balustrades. It is light and not
heavy in design with a warm, almost pink/terracotta brickwork
contrasting with the white stone edges. Bovolo means 'snail' due to the
spiral shape of the shell. The staircase winds and winds upwards in a
round spiral pattern. It gives a round tower and loggias on each floor
and a round covered loggia on the top floor. This has incredible views

across the city. It is 5 stories high and the two highest levels are shorter, designed to give the illusion that the tower is taller than it is.

At the top loggia you can see across the Venetian rooftops to San Marco Square. If you get there as the bells are about to ring then you will have several minutes as each bell (some early and some late) ring out across the city. Noon is a good time to be on the covered level looking out across Venice to the soundscape of its bells.

I find the courtyard at the base of the tower intriguing with stone well covers and troughs in an unkept grassy area. Even in December this gave an unusual small green space.

 *Momento di Mindfulness*
La Scala

If you go up the staircase then the views at the top, framed by the white stone arches, are a place to pause, focus and look out across the rooftops with mindfulness. Nothing more - it's absorbing in itself.

As you descend the staircase look out of each archway to the buildings which are so close-by, yet given an illusion of distance by the framed arches.

If it is closed and you are unable to go inside then it is still worth going and looking up at it from outside. You can look up towards the top. The grassy area and stone well covers/troughs are in my own mindful photo collection.

I never expected to find a small green space in December in that busiest part of Venice.

Ground Floor – Going up

There was a specific design pattern to the Medieval Palazzos. Due to the external staircase this is more clearly defined at the Bovolo but the design was similar for all Palazzos. They had a main entrance and boat dock on the canal and a second entrance in a calle at the back. The Ground Floor was usually the storage area. The next level was Mezzanino where the offices and daily business took place. Then going up a level to the Noble Floor where guests were received (and where

124

you are most likely to find the chandeliers). Further up still would be the family bedrooms and then the servants quarters. Each Palazzo stretched over 4 or 5 floors. At sky level there might be a Loggia or roof terrace. In recent years the number of roof terraces has grown and if you look up you will often see a 'rickety tickety' terrace. People want to sit out and gaze at the view and some days they might even catch a glimpse of the Dolomites in the distance.

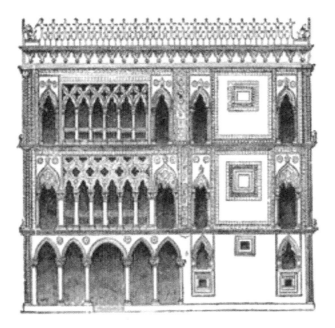

Luminous, Lugubrious, Lagoon Landscape

If you fly into Marco Polo airport you will see the marshy reeds of the lagoon as the aircraft lands and taxis to its stand. The flat marshy landscape where fresh water merges with salt water. In the distance you might see the outline of Venice or the Adriatic Sea.

The water of the lagoon merging into islets of marshes of reeds, sand and soil. This is what the landscape looked like before Venice was made habitable.

It is a wondrous landscape. If you arrive by bus or train then you do need to take a boat (a vaporetto or the Alilaguna) out into the lagoon at some point.

If you look towards the sea from the airport you will see the tower of the Basilica on the island of Torcello standing out in the lagoon landscape. In the summer it stands starkly against the sun filled landscape and in the winter it may rise out of the mists or dense fog of the lagoon.

The Laguna has scattered wooden posts marking the watercourses to help navigation keep to specific safe channels. In the marshy waters the water level can change suddenly and boats can go aground. You may see a 'dredger type boat' maintaining and replacing the posts as they decay in the saltwater. It's a never ending task keeping these posts repaired. Look out for a seabird resting on top of a post - it's a frequent site.

I love the lagoon landscape. Closer to and along the river which flows into the lagoon you can see the large square nets of the fishermen. Sometimes you can see other types of fishermen wading in shallow water to collect shellfish. It's alive and the fisherfolk continue the skills of centuries gone by. Did Marco Polo bring back those square nets you see along the river on the road to Jesolo?

Laguna is an ecosystem where those muddy shelves, above and below its waters are incredibly important. Venice is that complex system of river water and sea water found in an estuary. It's islands, it's houses built on wooden piles and towards the edge of the lagoon the fishing villages of Burano and further afield Palestrina. Close to the lagoon edge are rice-fields (risotto is a Venetian dish). The contrast between shallow water and deep channels means no area is the same and it is a lifetime skill to know how to pilot a boat safely across the lagoon. This living lagoon landscape is as vital as the brilliantly individual palazzi, churches and basilicas. The Magistrato alle Acque is responsible for maintaining the ecology of Venice and the lagoon.

The lagoon has islands which have served as market gardens for centuries. Mazzorbo and Sant' Erasmo.

It's impossible not to mention the industrial chemical plant of Porto Marghera. This can be seen in the distance from the Giudecca Canal. Work is underway to re-site the cruise and Greek Ferry terminal to a site away from the city.

In recent years the landscape on the journey by ferry to the port of Punta Sabboni has changed as it now passes close to part of the building of the MOSE Barriers. Following a scandal the date for completion of these flood defences has been delayed until 2022. MOSE consists of barrier gates which move and cut off the lagoon from the Adriatic when the tides are high. The scheme is designed to give protection to the city from high tides of up to 3 metres. There are 3 barriers at Lido, Chioggia and Malamocco where there are channels out of the lagoon. Will it give protection from the high tides of Acqua Alta?

Momento di Mindfulness
Ever changing shifting sands

The uninhabited islands of the lagoon are truly shifting sands. Think about the concept of 'shifting sands'. There are several inspirational quotes about adapting to life and changes such as 'learn to dance on a moving carpet' or 'dance in the rain'. Shifting sands give no certainty so we need to cope with the everchanging landscape of our life. The positive viewpoint here is that the Venetians worked with the shifting sands and created foundations which lasted. Yes, the wooden poles on which the houses are built and the canals need continual attention and renewal but there is a strong enough foundation to uphold the city.

Consider the foundations in your own life, your core values or faith, those people you care about, your commitments to others and any work you do. Those core values, the people we love 'ground us' and give a firm foundation to life. Imagine a movie screen in front of you and imagine written words for your values on banners moving across the screen. Some words will come straight into your thoughts and move across the screen. There may well be a couple of surprise words in there. We may live with our values but we don't always stop and consider what those values actually are. Take time to do that today – knowing your core values will be another holiday souvenir.

Wetland Habitat and Birdlife
I was fascinated to recently discover that there are strong ecological similarities between the Camargue and Venice. It is obvious if you think about it, I just never had. Laguna is the largest wetland habitat in Italy. The lagoon has an incredible range of birds, some migratory and the numbers have been rising steadily in the last thirty years due to conservation strategies.

The tide enters the lagoon and creates an even more unusual environment. The marshland has varying salt levels in its water depending how close it is to the river or the sea side of the lagoon. The network of channels, narrow shelved sandflats, swampy islands is unique for birdlife. The lagoon-scape near Pallestrina out towards Choggia is much more like the open sea, contrasting with the lagoon at the other side near to Torcello gives still brackish shallows.

Some of the birds you can see are surprising. There are many different types of ducks, seagulls, wading birds and, shore line birds. I was surprised to find there are heron as I'd thought they were river and freshwater birds. There are also cormorants, reaching Eastern Europe and Scandinavia. There are even now a number of flamingos which previously migrated from Tunisia to France and Sardinia but now stay in the lagoon. This does start to sound very like the Camargue and it is a side of Venice of which most visitors will be unaware and miss.

Momento di Mindfulness
Sounds of the Sea

Look out for gulls sitting on wooden posts way out on the lagoon. You will always see birds 'pausing on posts' from a boat.

Listen for the 'Sound of the Seagulls' as you walk along the Fondamenta or the Lido beach.

For me the memories and noise of the gulls calling 'in unison' is a sign I'm near the coast. It is the sound of the seaside.

The Bora
Cold as ice. The Bora is a winter wind which can sweep down over the city. The Bora happens when an area of polar high pressure sits over mountains with calm low pressure over the warmer Adriatic. As the air grows colder and denser at night the Bora becomes stronger.

There are two kinds of Bora, 'light bora' with clear skies and 'dark bora' with clouds from the hillside rolling down towards the sea with icy rain or snow. Bora Chiara and Bora Scura.

This northerly Bora wind is damp and chilling. It feels sub-zero even if it isn't.

A different kind of Delta
On the main islands near Rialto the population steadily grew. Small islands with narrow canals between them. Houses built closely together to maximise the space. Rainwater collected, crops grown, livestock farmed and a peaceful existence away from invasion and conflict.

Around the city the open water, the green, blue, silvery, grey changing colours of the lagoon. A lagoon which was part sea, lake and estuary formed by slow moving rivers reaching the sea. The estuary with its swampland, fresh water merging with the salt water and moving sluggishly to the sea, forming rivulets of fresh water merging into a salty lake like lagoon

The Brenta and Piave Rivers form this estuary with its unique delta landscape. Rivulets of fresh water and tidal salt water giving that varied ecological system. Marsh landscape with reeds, tough grassy fenland. Both fresh and saltwater fish adapting and living in the unique waters. There are tiny shrimp which are only found in the Venetian lagoon. Marsh creatures and migrating birds living on the grassy islands.

Saltpans emerged naturally from the shallow sand banks and the early Venetians realised that here was a source of income and began working with the landscape to develop commercial salt production. Oysters thriving and so becoming cultivated oyster beds. A plentiful source of crabs and shellfish in the salty mudbanks.

Navigating the waters of Laguna needed years of experience to avoid ships running aground so close to home. Developing skills of engineering to prevent the channels silting up with watermen skilled at dredging, patching seawalls, driving in replacement poles. Chilling winds sweeping down in the winter, hot baking islands in the summer. Swirling, spray filled waters and still limpid brackish pools.

The ceremony of the Marriage of the Sea is symbolic of a people who 'looked around them' and worked with their landscape to create wealth and comfort. It should have been impossible to build a city in this harsh environment.

 Momento di Mindfulness
Alto Adige, Monte Peralba & Pianura Padana

The Brenta and Piave Rivers formed the delta and lagoon. Where do these rivers have their sources and what is their course? Here some of the names of the places on the river routes. As I read them they seem almost like a mantra of soothing consonants and vowels. Names like Alto Adige, Monte Peralba, Valsugana and Pianura Padana flow together in linguistic beauty.

The Brenta flows for 108 miles. Its source is high up in Alto Adige in the mountains near Caldonazzo and Levico Lakes, it flows through Valsugana to Bassano del Grappa and is then joined by the Cismon, the Bacciglione and finally through the Pianura Padana and into the sea near Chioggia.

The Piave flows for 147 miles from the eastern Carnic Alps on the slopes on Monte Peralba, down through Belluno, Treviso and into the lagoon and the Adriatic near Cortellazzo between Eraclea and Jesolo. Near the mouth there is the Laguna del Mort formed by an old branch of the river.

Write a list or word web using the names of the places on the river routes. Choose the words where you like the sound pattern. Say the words to yourself in your head in a repetitive sequence so you have made another Venetian mantra. Imagine the high Alps where the rivers have their sources, the lakes and valleys on the journey to the sea.

Use the river journey as a metaphor for a difficult day or week. The journey is long and the river flows relentlessly onwards until it slows to a slow, steady pace as it reaches and merges with sea water in Laguna. The warm, sheltered waters of the lagoon.

Keep your word list with you. If you are travelling light then take a photo of your word web so that you can use it when you return home.

Part 8

MID AFTERNOON

"It is the city of mirrors, the city of mirages, at once solid and liquid, at once air and stone."

Erica Jon

Pause at a Water Fountain

'Water, water everywhere but not a drop to drink.' But not in Venezia! In Venice there is a network of drinking fountains. If you take an empty water bottle out with you, or a vacuum flask with ice cubes in it, then you will be able to replenish your container lots of times. There are at least a hundred drinking fountains in the city. The water is safe to drink and is continually sampled and tested. There even are maps online which show the location of the drinking fountains.

 *Momento di Mindfulness*
Cool Water

When you find a water fountain make filling your bottle a mindful moment. No one will notice if you do each step in a slow and steady way and take those slow and steady breaths as you fill the bottle and then take a drink.

Even if you don't have a water bottle there is nothing to stop you testing the fountain or even just putting your hand over the stream and feeling the cool water while you momentarily close your eyes.

In Search of ... Hidden Gardens

As you wander through the calles or sail up the canals you will very quickly notice trees and shrubs behind high walls and wrought iron fences. It's another hidden garden. However if you do an online search looking for hotels in Venice 'with gardens' there are very few results. And yet ... there are clearly many hidden green spaces in La Serenissima.

You are walking along a calle in San Polo or Santa Croce passing tall walls with worn bricks in muted shades. You are wandering into a dark Sottoportego (a passageway which goes underneath houses) which then emerges into a sun-filled calle. Behind a high brick wall you suddenly see trailing fronds of green ivy, lavender wisteria or white Jasmine. Then you spy an interior courtyard behind a wrought iron gate and see a stone pot on an internal stone stairway overflowing with geraniums and ivy spilling out. From a vaporetto you notice a gazebo covered with climbing clematis plants. There are green spaces everywhere.

There are some specialist walking tours to visit hidden gardens and these are not difficult to locate. There is also a rather special organisation which champions both restoring and promoting awareness of special historical gardens (the curiously named Wigwam Association). It seems there is a lot happening in the gardening world in Venice.

Mariagrazia Dammicco is a key name in Venetian garden conservation and development. She has made it a vocation to track and record the treasury of green spaces in the city. In her book *'A Guide to the Gardens of Venice'* Mariagrazia showcases about sixty Venetian gardens. The Wigwam Association has a website giving details about the heritage restoration programmes currently underway. Historic gardens are being restored and conserved for the future.

What sort of gardens are we talking about? Below are some examples but the list is long and it would certainly be possible to base a short break around the theme of 'Giardini Venezia'.

In the tours linked to the non-profit Wigwam Association 'you can enter aristocratic buildings, immerse yourself in the silence of ancient convents, reach parks lapped by the lagoon, meet the Venetians who still cultivate the gardens.' It's worth seeking out Mariagrazia's book and the website and visiting some secret gardens.

Easily Accessible Green Spaces
Here are some suggestions of places to visit. You may find you pass close-by one of these gardens when you are 'out and about'. It's a perfect reason to stop and pause. The earlier section on cloisters also contains suggestions for exploring green and serene spaces.

Venissa vineyard
There is a vineyard on the Island of Mazzorbo. It's a walled garden area and something of a conservation project. During the great flood of 1966 most of the fields in the lagoon were destroyed by the inundation of salt water. Eighty eight vines were saved from the deluge. These were planted at different

locations around the lagoon. Some are on Torcello. On Mazzorbo the sweet golden grapes of the Dorona vine were planted and are now made into Venissa wine. The wine is made by the Bisol family, hailing from the famous wine making area of Valdobbiadene (Valpolicella and Prosecco). The vineyard is thriving and now being called the Venissa Wine Resort.

There is now a restaurant and a small hotel at Venissa.
From the vaporetto stop at Mazzorbo you will see the Campanile of San Michele Archangelo if you look towards the left. You can walk through the vineyard area and vegetable garden. This short and tranquil walk gives you a totally different perspective on lagoon life. The vineyard might have been there in Roman or Medieval times.

Thetis garden

This is a sculpture garden at the Arsenale. Mostly people miss it and walk right past it. Thetis' garden is described as a 'hidden green oasis'. On weekdays, you can visit free of charge via the Bacini or Arsenale Nord vaporetto stop. I don't know this Bacini stop and research suggests it is on the number 5.2 vaporetto route but only 'on request'. You can also walk to the garden on the metal walkway attached to the walls of the Arsenale (which sounds fun). This walkway is now on my own list for my next visit to Venice.

Thetis' garden has sculptures. One sculpture is the 'Man who Measures the Clouds' by Belgian Jan Fabre. This garden can be a little overgrown depending on the time of year. Some wilder climbers might even be beginning to clamber over some of the sculptures. However this green wildness gives a mindful natural atmosphere. This untidy aspect may change as the garden is one of the projects undergoing restoration linked to the Wigwam Association.

Giardini Reali

This compact green space is very close to San Marco and pretty much at the San Marco vaporetto stop. The garden tends to be hidden behind the easels of artists and stalls selling souvenirs. As you walk from San Marco towards the vaporetto stop the garden is on your right. This garden was one of Napoleon's town planning initiatives. He wanted to use a building behind it as a palace with this as the garden area. The garden design was formal with knot patterned flower beds and paths.

In 1815, a greenhouse and a small pavilion, the Padiglione del Caffè, were added. Later a wrought iron pergola was built. In the early twentieth century the Giardini Reali area was given to the city council and became a public park. Until a couple of years ago the Tourist Information Office was in the Padiglione del Caffe (Coffee House). Over time this garden became a place to sit and rest, eat a packed lunch or as a meeting point for groups. It became faded and dated in design. It had seen better days.

The garden has been closed for restoration and is scheduled to open again very soon. The plan was to restore the Giardini Reali so it was closer to the original design. There has been research into the original planting scheme. Not only the garden but the wrought iron pergola, coffee house, greenhouse and mini drawbridge have been restored.

The flowerbed planting will consist of drifts of Iris, Agapanthus, Hibiscus Rosa-Sinensis (Chinese roses), Hydrangeas and Camelias. New evergreen small Magnolias, and the unusual Tetrapanax Papyrifer (or Chinese rice paper) with its rhubarb -like grey leaves. In the spring daffodils and tulips will give vibrant colour. The restored pergola will be covered with an original species of Wisteria. The restored Giardini Reali have the potential to be a special tranquil green space in the middle of the busiest area of Venice.

Festival dei Giardini
The Wigwam Club Giardini Storici Venezia was set up in 2000. The objective is to increase the awareness and appreciation of historical gardens. One event initiated by the organisation is the Festival dei Giardini which takes place on the first weekend in October.
It's fast become a yearly tradition. A selection of the most hidden courtyards and gardens (often usually closed to the public) are opened up for visitors. Volunteers organise walking tours, talks by gardeners, authors, performances, all showcasing the historical background and features of the selected secret gardens of Venice.

Guggenheim Garden
This is not as hidden as the others but is still a cool oasis during a day of sightseeing. Peggy Guggenheim settled in Venice at the Palazzo Venier dei Leoni on the Grand Canal. When the art collection opened in 1949 the sculpture garden was very much a central focus. Today you can still experience this unusual tranquil garden.

Walls are covered with ivy interspersed with illuminated neon statements. Spindly sculptures rise up among the trees. In this artistic nature trail you will discover works by Henry Moore, Marino Marini and Alberto Giacometti. You will also notice the graves of both Peggy and fourteen of her dogs ('beloved babies'). This garden is also known as the Nasher Sculpture Garden.

Momento di Mindfulness
Curating a collection of green spaces

Curate a Collection of your own Green Spaces in Venice. Take photos of unexpected greenery. A hidden courtyard with a climbing plant. A scented rose in a cloister. A window box filled with vibrant Geranium and Begonias. Another 'memory bank', with a different theme, is created for you to browse when you return home.

Cedar & Cypress – Seeking Shade
Sometimes on a hot day in Italy there is almost a scent of pine tree in the air. Pine oil is resinous, with a strong woody fragrant smell. It's been described as rather like pencil shavings mixed with camphor.

There are many cypress and cedar trees in the lagoon. San Michele is bordered by a ring of Cypress trees. There are pine trees in the Giardini Gardens.

There is another small park near Piazzale Roma very near the bus station in Santa Croce. Sometimes you can almost smell the cedar and cypress trees. It's called the Giardini Papadopoli park.

Nestling in a corner between two canals and just over the footbridge from Piazzale Roma this small botanical garden and playground has been there since 1834. It was designed and driven by Francesco Bagnara. Interesting because Francesco was a set painter at La Fenice who went on to teach at the Accademia. The garden is on the site of the demolished convent of Santa Croce.

The paths wind around planted beds with Cypress, Cedar, Oleander and Laurel. In the 19th century there were rare flowers and shrubs in the beds and these gardens were the setting for society soirées. It became faded and neglected over time Then a third of the Giardino was taken in 1933 in a city planning development involving the construction of Rio Nuovo canal and a new hotel.

There has been some work to restore Giardino Papadopoli with repaired walls, gates and paving stones. Now it is an oasis of calm. There is hope it will be maintained and not become neglected again.

Momento di Mindfulness
Bring Balm to tired feet

Venice is the city for walking. Feet can falter. Tired feet need attention. They need to feel refreshed and revived to keep up the momentum of further walking. Find some lotion with a fragrance you like. Spread your feet out on a towel and spend 5 minutes giving your feet a gentle mindful massage. Spend time massaging lotion into your feet. Take your time. Make it last as a mindful moment. Bring 'balm' to tired, aching feet.

If you can, then before you massage your feet with lotion why not soak your feet in warm water with just a few drops of an essential oil like Geranium, Lavender or Peppermint added. Depending where you are staying a hotel bidet can certainly be brought into action for soaking tired feet.

Tiramisu, Zabaione & Fritelle

There is something about the experience of eating Tiramisu, well known as 'the Venetian Dessert' which counts as mindfulness. Marscapone is one of those foods which cannot be eaten quickly and surely needs to be eaten slowly and savoured. It's included in the lunchtime/afternoon section because this gives opportunity to 'walk off the calories mindfully' with another long walk.

The translation of Tiramisu is literally 'pick me up' and 'make me happy' in local Venetian terms. It's not an ancient recipe. It seems to have dated from the late 1960s (though that is disputed). The creation is credited to Roberto Linguanotto, Chef at the Beccherie restaurant in Treviso. The mixture of marscapone, cream, sponge, chocolate and often Marsala wine 'just works'. We recently saw a Tiramisu making machine in a restaurant in Dorsoduro. It was a little like a coffee machine with coffee machine type buttons for each step of the process. Fascinating - but definitely not how I want my Tiramisu made.

Interestingly one of the highest rated Tiramisu is at a Pasticceria and not a restaurant. It's Pasticceria Tonolo in Calle San Pantalon. The bakery/café is highly rated for its coffee and tiramisu. They seem to have a secret ingredient in their zabaione cream!

Fritelle are small, soft, fried filled doughnuts. Fritelle are usually only eaten at Carnivale, though it's increasingly possible to get something similar at other times of the year.

The doughnuts are usually filled with Zabaglione and that's with plenty of marsala in the mixture. They resemble choux pasty and are quite soft. Variations are Veneziane where the dough is enriched with raisins and pine nuts but has no cream and 'con crema' with vanilla custard cream.

The Tonolo Pasticceria in Dorsoduro is famous for its Fritelle con zabaione. Rosa Salve in Calle Fiubera in Castello is equally noteworthy. There will, of course, be many other places to call and take this seasonal pastry with a cappuccino.

 Momento di Mindfulness
Hope & Happiness

Tiramisu is literally the 'make me happy dessert'. Happiness and hopefulness go together. So here is a way of remembering some key aspects of mindfulness using the letters of the word 'Hope'.

Happy in the 'here-and-now' moment
Observe
Pause & Practice
Energy & Engage

Be Happy & Hopeful on Holiday

Siesta in La Serenissima

When I was a child visiting Italy the shops always closed for the afternoon. There was a long closure from 12.30/13:00 hrs to about 16:00 hrs. We waited eagerly for the shops to open again (usually hoping for ice cream or crisps) Everywhere seemed to shut for the afternoon.

Then gradually over the years the shops started to open for longer and the traditional siesta shortened. In Venice it's now mostly now non-existent. In those days there were no Supermercatos, only the small neighbourhood Alimentare with a uniquely wonderful Italian smell of cheese, salami and Parma ham permeating the shop.

France still adheres quite strictly to its 90 minute lunch break but it seems quite eroded in Italy. You can still walk through the streets and smell lunch cooking through the open windows of the calles. However it is rare to find a shop which closes for the afternoon.

Whatever the time of year try to make it a routine to return to your hotel at some point in the afternoon and take a 'siesta'. What could be more mindful than a culture giving the opportunity for a structured mindfulness mediation in the afternoon? Thirty minutes of rest and rejuvenation of tired feet and body. Make it multi-sensory experience and start with a cup of tea.

Momento di Mindfulness
Tea time and Mindful Meditation

Whatever the time of year you are going to need a break from walking round. It can be very refreshing to return to your hotel or apartment and take a short siesta (aka power nap).

Make yourself a drink of tea. I suggest chamomilla (chamomile) tea, but choose something you enjoy. Lie down and rest. You may fall asleep of course, but even just resting and working through a body scan meditation should refresh and restore your energy levels for the rest of the day.

The website of Mindful Magazine has a script for a Body Scan Meditation which lasts 3 minutes. There is an accompanying audio from the magazine's website or via UCLA's Mindfulness Awareness Research Center (MARC) . There is also an audio on the website longer

45 minute Body Scan from UC San Diego Center for Mindfulness which is used in its Mindfulness-Based Stress Reduction training. Many other audio versions are available on sites like Tara Brach's or the various Apps for mindfulness. These two are signposted as suggestions for those who may not have their favourite audio version of a body scan meditation.

You can also try the *'Tension into Relaxation'* meditation if this approach suits you. *'Tension into Relaxation'* can be very valuable at all times of the day when muscles are feeling tired and makes sure your whole body is relaxed.

Opposites - Tension dissolving into Relaxation
Sit or lie down. Close your eyes.

Notice any thoughts hovering in the background but do no more than that. Just notice the thoughts. Hopefully they will be fleeting and flit off into the distance as you notice them.

Go through each parts of your body in sequence. Start with your shoulders as these often hold tension. Squeeze your shoulders backwards (tense them), hold for a second or two and then let go and relax. Move your shoulders in gently up and down or in a rotating movement.

Move from the shoulder down your arm to your elbow and do the same again. Tense then relax. Then the forearm and then the hands and fingers. Tense, hold briefly and relax.

Go through your whole body in sequence – chest, abdomen, legs and feet. Right down to your toes.

When you get to your neck very gently tense and release those muscles. Gently rotate your neck.

Focus on your jaw which can often be held tightly and make sure your teeth are apart and your tongue is not held tightly against the roof of your mouth. Work through your cheeks, forehead in the same way. Tense gently and relax.

Finally just imagine letting your brain, let your thinking go limp. Hold the base of your skull at the back of your neck and support your head with both hands. Let your thoughts soften and feel a sinking sensation as thoughts dissolve and you relax.

Spend a few minutes with your body and thoughts feeling soft loose and relaxed. Now you need to recharge your energy.

Gently starting to move the different parts of your body. Move your fingers and toes, rock gently backwards and forwards. Slowly open and close your eyes several times. Gentle movements to generate energy in your body ready for another walk.

Mindful Maravege
Over the years we had stayed in a few places in Venice. On one occasion it was in apartment which was the least expensive we could find which had a terrace. It was in the furthest reaches of Castello, though quite conveniently close to the Arsenale vaporetto stop. On another occasion we booked an expensive hotel on the Riva degli Schiavoni which had a stupendous view of Palladio's church on San Giorgo but was marred by the continuous bass beat of the music from a souvenir stall which was wheeled into position every morning just beneath our window. The fraying stair carpet and the dull breakfast room were not inspiring. For a special Wedding Anniversary we stayed at the Locanda Vivaldi on the Riva which was lovely and we had a room with several windows and amazing views onto the Bacino and which had the advantage of being very close to the ferry terminal.

Then one day we were walking through Dorsoduro from Rialto to Accademia when I saw what looked like a hotel with a garden. We walked up the canal to the very end of the path to a wrought iron gated archway with sign saying Villa Maravege. My partner walked right through the gate and into the garden. I hesitated then followed. Inside there was a garden on the canal, with places to sit under a shaded gazebo. There was place to eat breakfast in a garden next to the canal. When we returned home I contacted the hotel and booked a room for a visit in a few months' time. I'd discovered what we now call 'The Pensione'; to give it its full title the Pensione Accademia/Villa Maravege.

The building has history. It's a seventeenth century Gothic style Palazzo which became the Russian Embassy between the world wars. Then it finally became a Pensione in 1950. It was a film set for part of a Katherine Hepburn movie called 'Summertime'. The movie was set in the 1950s with a story about a holiday romance.

On arrival at the Pensione I discovered there was a second internal courtyard garden. A long covered arch, even sun loungers on a grassy lawn amid lovely trees and flowers. A haven of tranquillity in the city. There is even a glimpse of the Grand Canal from some of the rooms.

We discovered the Pensione on that warm spring day in the late afternoon. The garden at the front was filled with flowers and quiet, peaceful tranquillity. It's a special place to which I've returned time and time again.

It's in the afternoon that we return here, after an inevitably long session walking to the far reaches of Venice. We may just sit under the shaded gazebo next to the canal, or sit at a table in the shade in the inner courtyard garden. We might drink the complimentary lemonade in the summer or the warm spicy tea in cooler weather. There is often a tea time Cicchetti snack and there is always fruit and sometimes that's all I've needed in the heat of the afternoon. Better to wait for the cooler evening to eat. Sometimes I go to the bar for a chamomilla tea or English tea with lemon. A long refreshing drink in the shade of a garden away from the dusty, parched calles of the city.

Then a short rest in the room, listening to sounds from outside, giving a mindful interlude before gearing up for the next session of exploring the visual treasures of the streets Venice

In the winter the fireplace sizzles with logs burning. It's a cosy place to pass an hour reading in front of the fire. The rooms have reproduction or vintage Venetian style furniture, we had a marquetry bureau. The public sitting area on the first floor is filled with antiques including a suit of armour and a sewing machine!

The room we had on our first visit gave us a canal view of the Rio San Trovarso Canal. I'd be woken with the unique Venetian soundtrack of passing delivery boats, firemen and the occasional gondola. Since then we've also stayed in a room looking over the garden filled with peace and quiet. To have breakfast in a garden looking out towards the Grand Canal with a fountain with a lion's head on the wall and sparrows waiting to swoop down for any crumbs is a lovely way to start the day.

The Pensione is a family owned hotel, the owner is often on the premises. The staff are friendly professional people who have mostly worked at the hotel during all the years we've been visiting. In a city like Venice this must be unusual. The Reception team, the cleaners and house staff and the gentleman who oversees the breakfast room. There is something special about being recognised when you go into the breakfast area with a "Come va?"and a remarkable memory, knowing that we prefer to have cappuccino instead of the Americano style coffee at breakfast. We know the staff's names, we email about a room, not because you can't book online, but because the personal touch in the reply somehow feels like the start of the holiday journey.

This reads a little like an advert and it isn't meant to be. It's more about showing that in a city which is often in the news for its considerable issues around being out of balance with too many tourists for its facilities there are still places like the Pensione where you can stay and support local employment and sustainable tourism. As I write this the first charge for day trippers is being introduced, along with other extreme measures like turnstiles limiting the number of people entering the Rialto and San Marco areas. The city is certainly considering drastic ways to improve the city environment.

Hotels like La Calcina on the Zattere look small and friendly, special places to stay. The Ca' Beatrice tea room has bed and breakfast rooms which look lovely on their website and I've seen guests there when I've been in the tea room. Antica Locanda Montin seems individual and has another beautiful garden for guests to take breakfast in the warmer weather. My brother has stayed on a small hotel which was pretty much on the Accademia Bridge, looking out from his room onto a view of the

Canale Grande. Within 500 metres of the Pensione there must be countless small and friendly places to stay. This will be true of every Sestiere.

I don't know the quiet Giudecca island well. It's somewhere I need to explore much more but I know there will be bed and breakfast and small hotels there (alongside the luxurious Molino Stucky Hilton and the Cipriani). I've often thought of staying a night at the Locanda Cipriano on Torcello to experience a different flavour of Lagoon life. The trouble is my favourite Pensione Accademia /Villa Maravege keeps drawing me back with its individual, quirky charm.

The Pensione has been described as 'spellbinding' and it's a very special atmospheric place. There is no lift so it is a 3 Star Hotel but with incredible individuality and character. After a day of walking many miles, returning to the garden to sit with a glass of prosecco or a chamomile tea makes for a perfect retreat. Wisteria and Sunshine. We all find different places we prefer and for me this is my mindful place in Venice. Marvellously Mindful Maravege.

 Momento di Mindfulness
Multi-sensory rules of listening

Focusing and listening to sounds in the environment around us is a way of calming and quietening a mind which might be busy with 'flitting' thoughts. Holiday thoughts are hopefully happy thoughts, but there are occasional moments when stress levels rise when travelling. Anticipating an early flight and travel arrangements perhaps. Once when we were away there was a planned strike the day we were leaving. It does happen. The connection with the 'soundscape' around you and giving focused attention to specific sounds diverts the brain from endless loops of worrying, planning and 'being busy". Listening is a route to breaking through to a racing mind, as sounds wash through our thoughts then our bodies relax.

Remember the Multi – Sensory Rules of Listening
Listen with your ears and your eyes too. Make a moment of listening into a more multi-sensory experience. Start with noticing the sounds you hear and mentally making a list. Perhaps it's a boat engine, a tap dripping or voices on the corridor.

146

Scent of Chamomilla – a pot of afternoon tea
If I have an cup of 'English' tea in Venice then I take it very weak with
a slice of lemon. I have it almost like flavoured hot water. A second pot
of water is helpful to prevent the tea from becoming too strong. At
home I drink very strong Assam English Breakfast tea. Even with an
additional teabag added to a pot is pretty much impossible to get tea as
'golden' as I like it in Italy. The closest I've got to it is a strong Orange
Pekoe from the supermercato.

However weak 'tea con limone' is refreshing and works well on a
warm day.

Sometimes I abandon English tea and ask for a pot of Chamomilla
instead. In Northern Italy Chamomile tea is often served in a small
teapot with an additional pot of water and some lemon slices. It's light,
refreshing and relaxing and lasts for a long time. I usually get at least 3
cups to my partners 1 cup of coffee!

After a morning of walking it's both reviving and hydrating.
Chamomilla can be drunk any time of day but I prefer it in the
afternoon.

If you're on a strict budget and have a kettle in your hotel room then
why not call in a supermarket and buy an inexpensive packet of
Chamomilla and a lemon. This will last you throughout your holiday
and also weighs nothing so you can take home as a souvenir.

Momento di Mindfulness
Scented treats

More multi-sensory suggestions for quiet contemplative moments.
Remember to breathe in the scent of your tea or coffee. Before you take
a sip then spend a few moments breathing in the scented steam.

Breath in the scent of drinks and snacks while you are our and about. If
you take a walk through a supermercato they are always different to the
ones at home. The supermercato is actually a great place to notice
differences and focus attention (who thought shopping could be
mindful …)

There is a scenic supermercato on the Zattere and you walk out to a
view across to the Mulino Stucky building on Guidecca. I often go
between noon and three o'clock when it is much quieter and I'm not

getting in the way of busy locals who are on their way to and from work.

Scented Treats:

Honey Sweets
Bacci Chocolates (hazelnut praline)
Marron glace
Soft Italian nougat
Watermelon
Almonds and walnuts
Peaches – large and dripping with juice and my favourite in August
Satsuma (in a paper wrapping) is my favourite in the winter
Hot Focaccia bread studded with garlic

Radiant Light & Colour – Bellini and Titian

In the BBC programme "Radiance" Simon Schama points out that in Venetian Renaissance paintings there is a "key role of colour and light". In Florence the artists took inspiration from 'outlines of contours of form'. In Venice the artists instead focused on light and colours; how different colour and light energy flowed between objects. How boundaries can be broken down or seem transparent. Bellini and Titian are seen as the originators of this Venetian 'colour based' tradition. Titian was Bellini's student so there is a strong link between them.

There must surely be more in the roots of this Venetian painting style than this scientific explanation of art history. The city and its unique location of the lagoon and the light and colour of an island must have been an influence. A living influence with rapidly changing skyscapes, water forming a flowing and ever changing backdrop to the colours of the buildings. Maybe this is why Titian and Bellini took this colour based approach to their artistic creations.

Bellini found and focused on golden light, some say with 'supernatural implications, as it illuminates the surfaces of bodies'. This would have given the medieval people a wondrous feeling of other worldliness and the serious reality of the closeness to heaven and death.

Titian painted in a style that was increasingly individual and personal to him. One witness describes how Titian sometimes abandoned his brush to get closer to the canvas or wall and actually paint with his fingers.

This gives insight to how Titian became joined to his work and how colour could be flowing, moving and separate from the underlying shape or form. This is expressive art.

Tom Nichols writes "in his hands, colour became something very different again: the means of describing the world as a place awash with sensual experience and emotion, open to sudden and unexpected change, and governed by the fluid subjectivity of human experience"

Was there competitiveness and even animosity between the master and his pupil ? It seems there was some competitiveness in later years. They were different in subtle yet were both in very strong ways influenced by the radiant golden light, colour and movement of their city.

Momento di Mindfulness
Lightness & Clarity

Find five minutes sitting down somewhere with 'a view'. Sit quietly and close your eyes briefly. Open your eyes again.

Focus on colour, shape and light. Make your vision go soft. Merging forms together in a Monet-type style. Changes in light levels. Bright sunshine and dimmer shady corners.

Lightness, Brightness & Clarity.

Now shine your attention inwards and onto something which is on your mind. Maybe something you are considering and unsure about, maybe about to make a decision about. Bring in a relaxed attitude of clarity, lightness and brightness and see if that makes you see it differently and closer to your decision.

Later, when you next walk around the city then notice the contrast and change in light and brightness when you move from a narrow calle into a light open campo or Riva. Blink purposefully and slowly and look again at the view.

Let your eyes rest on the different colours and shape. See the colours in your mind's eye and commit to that memory bank.

Look to the sides and what you can see in your peripheral vision. You will notice something different if you look to the periphery.

Afternoon Island Hopping

Bustling Burano
The Number 12 vaporetto line runs from Venice to Isola di Burano. Larger ferries go from San Zaccaria or Fondamenta Nuove to Burano and Murano. It takes about 40 minutes to reach Burano.

Burano is a place where some of the most skilled boatmen with in depth knowledge of the tides and currents of the lagoon come from. Those who have read Donna Leon's novels will appreciate the skills of Bonsuan and Foa, the pilots of the police launches which take Brunetti the Commissario and his colleague Vianello around Venice and across the lagoon. The island of Burano is a fishing village, hence the renowned navigation skills of the fishermen.

Jan Morris describes Burano as "a sheer splash of colour". It's a lovely, apt description The houses might individually seem garish but combined together they mingle and merge into that vivid canvas of colour. The houses are brighter and more vibrant than in Venice itself. These are not palazzos but fisherman's cottages. Sometimes you will see the washing hanging outside to dry. Folklore says that the houses were painted brightly so the fishermen could see them from a long way out on the lagoon. A beacon to guide them home. Some of the best fish dishes in Venice can be found at restaurants on Burano.

Other aspects of Burano are the traditional lacemaking. Is there a link between the skills of lacemaking and fishing and mending nets? Who knows? Burano was a centre for lace from the 16th century. Each woman had skills in just a single stitch. The Burano form of lacemaking has seven stitches. Each piece would be passed along to seven women who added their stitch. A lace insert for the centre of a handmade tablecloth might take four weeks to complete. The Museo del Merletto or Lace Museum in the Civic Hall is the place to go to find out more about this unique craft.

If you are going to browse souvenir shops then Burano is a good place for it. You may find authentic lace or like me choose an inexpensive fan with a lace insert, which wasn't made on the island. However the souvenir shop will have hopefully contributed to the island income and the authentic lace is, of course, expensive.

The bell tower is leaning and it's significantly leaning. It isn't the Leaning Tower of Pisa but you can take the same sorts of 'funny photos' where you lean over.

Moments in Mazzorbo

If you wander over the Ponte Longo and across to the neighbouring island of Mazzorbo look out for glimpses of the lagoon and seagulls. Where there are fish there will surely be gulls. Mazzorbo is another world where the focus is on growing artichokes, fruit in orchards and a vineyard.

Mazzorbo has a growing reputation for gastronomy. Some years ago I watched the British TV Chef Jamie Oliver in Venice cooking a Risotto in a restaurant on this island. Risotto is very Venetian dish. We still use this recipe at home. Jamie makes a basic risotto base and only adds the specific flavouring towards the end of cooking e.g. mushrooms and sage, chicken and thyme, asparagus and parmesan.

Alternatively it's worth getting off the boat from Venice at Mazzorbo and walking across to Burano. You will miss any summer crowds 'piling off' your crowded boat at the Burano stop. You will feel very close to the lagoon here. Walk through this quieter island with vineyards and an old monastery then go over a wooden bridge and you are in bustling, busy Burano.

Momento di Mindfulness
Memories of long ago ice cream

My childhood memory of Burano and Mazzorbo is not of the fishing boats or the lace making. My memory is of the ice cream! Perhaps we had a long time on the island and it was hot and I was tired. It was therefore one of the most wonderful ice creams ever. Think back to your own favourite 'ice cream moments'. My Burano ice cream is rivalled only by the soft vanilla & lemon cones made by Pacitos on the Foreshore of a North Yorkshire seaside resort called Scarborough.

Buy an ice cream from somewhere close to the vaporetto stop. Eat it as 'slow food' on your slow travel visit to Burano. Taste, texture and temperature. Taste slowly and savour your ice cream.

Time in Torcello

"You should choose the finest day in the month and have yourself rowed far away across the lagoon to Torcello. Without making this excursion you can hardly pretend to know Venice".

Henry James "An early impression" in Italian Hours

A small ferry runs from Burano to Torcello every 30 minutes. There are many guided tours to the island. These usually go to Murano, Burano and on to Torcello. These tours are a convenient, easy way to visit the islands and can usually be booked at your hotel or at the vaporetto stop at San Marco. You will easily find a tour of 'the islands'. If you go alone then you have the option of choosing a quieter time of day. If you have time to explore Torcello independently then you will have a different, more solitary, island experience. Both the tour and independent approach are worthwhile ways of seeing this island and I've done both more than once.

Torcello is the most northerly of the inhabited islands. If you have longer than 3 days in Venice then a journey across the lagoon to the island of Torcello is always special. If you are spending Mindful Days in Venice then it should be high on your list of places to visit.

I find it hard to believe that Torcello was once the centre of Venice back in the fifth century. In the 10th century Torcello was a significant political and trading centre with at least 3,000 (some estimates say around 20,000) people living there. The lagoon waters were harvested for salt which was exported from its thriving harbour area. Whether due to plague, silted lagoon or malaria the population dwindled away.

It's now a place where the lagoon landscape is in control. Glimpses of flat reedy salt marsh with occasional seabirds and a wild lagoon which seems to go on forever.

Ruskin writes about "the throat-catching beauty and loneliness of ruined Torcello" describing "a waste of wild sea moor... a lurid ashen grey" where nothing survives but two churches, some gravestones, a bell tower and a few inns.

Nowadays Torcello has a few farmhouses and restaurants and a small hotel the Locanda Cipriani It has an 'away from it all', occasionally eerie feeling.

Leave the boat and get your bearings. Look back at the lagoon and the views towards Burano and the empty stretches of lagoon. Set off and walk along the long pathway alongside a still canal. See grass and scrubland and the occasional house. You will come across the Devil's Bridge (supposedly built by the Devil in one night to win a bet). It has no sides and is one of only two bridges in Venice like this. Walk a little further and come to another bridge leading to a small simple campo.

The campo is still entirely made of clay and gravel. Sometimes in the high season there are some souvenir stalls towards the side. One of the sites is a famous marble throne, sometimes called Attila's Throne, but thought to have been used by the Bishop of Torcello. It's usually a photo opportunity.

Most special of all is the Basilica of Santa Maria Assunta dating from 639. It was rebuilt in the year 1008. It has a vast wall of mosaic images. The influence of eastern Byzantium is strong. The mosaics tell the story of the crucifixion and imagines the rising of the dead on the Day of Judgement. This enormous picture of the trials and tribulations awaiting humanity is compelling even today. The mosaic of the Madonna was made by Greek craftsmen in an Orthodox style.

Visitors can now go down to the crypt under the altar, going through a passage where you can see the bricks of the original Basilica. The campanile is often the first site you see from Marco Polo Airport. You can climb the campanile for the views of the island and onwards to the endless marsh and mudflats of the lagoon.

Wander into the ancient octagonal church of Santa Fosca, which is surrounded by a loggia/portico.

Towards the left is the Palazzo del Consiglio, *Consiglio (parliament house)* and the *Palazzo dell'Archivio (archives)*. These palazzos form the Torcello museum. The museum has archaeological discoveries from the post Roman, Byzantine and Medieval times.

Jan Morris writes about Torcello as a place of "lethargy and despondence, deserted and disused, rotting and declining into marshland". Centuries before the Venetians had loaded the remains of the 'decayed' palazzos onto barges, taking them to Venice to be recycled into new palazzos. Morris visited in the years following the end of the second world war. I visited in the early 1970s and have been back many times since then.

The island always draws me back. It is an eerie, tranquil flatland. Yes, the island is mostly deserted now and on a hot day the heat walking from the boat to the Basilica can be intense. However for me there is a contemplative, spiritual quality to the island as you follow its wide canal with the Ponte del Diavolo, (Devil's Bridge) leading to the small cluster of buildings in the square. The untidiness of the grassy, gravelly campo gives a change after the paved, structured architectural campos of Venice.

Jan Morris also writes of "exquisite nostalgia" of distant campanile and "haunted waterways". On Torcello you will find echoes of the past and unique and absorbing mosaic images in an ancient cathedral.

 *Momento di Mindfulness*
Slow Travel is surely here!

The whole visit to Torcello might count as a mindful experience. From the moment you leave the small ferry and walk along the pathway to the small square. Sit on the Throne of Attila and feel the coolness of the marble.

Choose an aspect of your visit on which to focus. It might be a view, part of the mosaic, a tree, some marble. Give full focused attention to whatever aspect you choose. Remember to breath and take slow and steady breaths. Is the air still or is there a breeze. Is the temperature hot, warm or colder?

When in the Basilica sit and look at the vast mosaic of the Day of Judgement or the Madonna against the gold leaf - or both. Notice the light and how it is different in the Basilica, notice especially any patterns of sunlight or shadows. Close your eyes and open them again.

For me the whole island visit is an opportunity for slow, mindful perception and thinking.

Make your time in Torcello a mindful memory.

San Francisco del Deserto

Away from Venice, to the east of Burano, is the monastery island
of San Francisco del Deserto. You are out on the lagoon landscape with
the mud flats and salt marsh. The sea air surrounds you but the lagoon
is mostly sheltered from the Adriatic. You are in the fenland of St
Francis. The mudflats and salt marsh are the home to seabirds and if
you look carefully the occasional heron. A place with cypress trees and
cobbled paths leading to a quiet sanctuary. There are views from the
western shore to Burano and Torcello.

Francis was here on the lagoon. The community of monks was founded
in 1230. The island is bordered by pine trees and cypress. The island
was abandoned at times in the early days due to malaria. When
Napoleon occupied Venice the island became a storage area with
gunpowder here. A long way from the gentle peaceful approach of the
Franciscan friars.

The island has green grassy areas and depending on the time of year
you visit may be filled with flowers. It is peaceful with an unusual
serene silence. The Friars who live here will welcome you to their
island and show you their truly tranquil cloisters.

My family smile because I am always intrigued by cloisters. Whether it
is one of the amazing Cistercian Abbeys near my home in North
Yorkshire, England like the awesome Rievaulx or Venetian cloisters
like the Friary, San Francesco dei Vigno or San Giorgio I tend to seek
them out. I like to wander through a cloister, feeling the history of the
setting, walking under the surrounding portico or loggia.

Many years ago on a rare March day in Rome at the Basilica of St Paul
Without the Walls, I first smelled the scent of boxwood, a resinous oil
and unique scent. I was hooked and went home and learned how to take
cuttings and propagate box.

Here on the island you find shady ancient cloisters. In the middle of the
cloister is a well from the 15th century which reaches down to a water
supply of rainwater collected in a cistern beneath the cloister.

There is a story about St Francis communicating with the wildlife on
the island. When St Francis arrived in 1220, the man he was travelling
with knelt down to give a prayer for their safe arrival. He was unable to
focus due to the loud singing of the birds. St Francis spoke with the

birds asking them to be quiet until the prayers were over. This story is depicted on a stone tablet near the church. Look out for the symbol of the Franciscan Order which is two crossed arms bearing stigmata. The arm of Christ and the arm of St Francis.

Near one of the chapels is a semi-fossilised pine tree. This pine tree is said to have grown from a stick planted by St Francis when he arrived on the island. When he did this the birds flocked to Francis to sing. The island is certainly alive with the spirit of St Francis.

This is a place to imagine the monks of the past 'prayerful and reflective' with 'cloisters old and serene' (Morris). Visiting the island needs a little effort to arrange. There are now some excursions to the island and it is becoming easier to hire a boat, perhaps even one of the historical wooden boats from Burano to San Francesco.

Look out for the tamarisk trees which grow well in this part of the lagoon. Some say this is the tree with the 'manna from heaven' which God gave to the desperate Moses and his people. Tamarisk trees were once extensive throughout southern Sinai. Their resin is unusual and resembles wax, melting when it grows warm in the sun, releasing a sweet and aromatic liquid. This liquid resembles yellow honey. This honey like resin fits with the Biblical descriptions of manna.

 *Momento di Mindfulness*
Silence & Tranquility

The path from the jetty is bordered by cypresses which give shade and beauty. Focus on the trees as you walk along the path. Imagine the centuries of monks walking along this path on their island haven.

Listen for the birds, or is it silent? Remember the story of St Francis talking to the birds and requesting their silence while a prayer took place. This is a place of tranquillity to treasure.

The Island of Sant' Erasmo

The Island of Sant' Erasmo is actually the largest individual island in the lagoon. It is also the quietest with the smallest population. There are around 750 people living here. This is the garden of Venice or market garden. It has a fertile soil and perfect microclimate.

In the baking hot summer heat Sant' Erasmo is a place to escape from the heat. Venetian families visit at the weekends to have a picnic on the 'Bacan' beach. There are two festivals on Sant' Erasmo - one to celebrate the purple artichoke and the other the local wine.

Sant' Erasmo Island shows a different sort of lagoon life. You can walk or cycle. It's a haven, an escape from the hot and crowded Venice. Nature surrounds you.

Sant' Erasmo is mentioned in ancient documents for their orchards. Other islands also had orchards. San Secondo, Torcello, Mazzorbo, Lio Maggiore, Ammiana, San Nicolò di Lido and the Giudecca.

Garlic, onions, leek, turnips, carrots available together with glasswort (or salicornia) that protected sailors against scurvy and still features in Rialto market as a special delicacy. And flowers like tulips, hyacinths, jasmine and carnations would grow there too.

Momento di Mindfulness
Calm Cues

This is a green and peaceful garden island. Sant' Erasmo is a haven of calm. Consider the letters of the word *CALM* and use as cues for a mindful moment.

Consider ... Absorb ... Look again ... Make it Mindful Moment

Consider what you see and hear around you. Close your eyes then look again. Notice anything different. Focus on the sights, sounds and atmosphere of the island.

Make this another mindful memory. Take photos to help you remember the day you left the beaten track for a visit to a different type of island

Sad Cypress on San Michele

> *"Come away, come away, death,*
> *And in sad cypress let me be laid"*
> *Shakespeare in Twelfth Night*

A ring of cypress trees surrounds the Island of San Michele. Before 1804 there were several cemeteries in Venice. Napoleon ordered that no one should be buried on the island for sanitary reasons. If you travel from the airport by boat then you will catch glimpses of the 'sad cypresses' of the cemetery island. If you walk along the Fondamenta Nuova by the hospital you will see the tree ringed island on the near horizon.

San Michele was originally inhabited by monks. The last monks left in 2008. One of the medieval monks was Fra Mauro. Fra Mauro never travelled but he had an interest in places far away. He was fascinated by the adventures of Marco Polo. He encouraged travellers who might stop off at the island to talk about the places they had visited. He listened, imagined and created a world map. This map is surprisingly detailed and can be seen at the Marciana Library in Piazza San Marco.

It's astounding that this simple monk, who never travelled himself, created the most important world map of the Middle Ages. He could be almost considered as the personification of Google Earth in the 15th century. As merchant adventurers came to Venice to buy and sell goods he asked them to share stories about the countries they had visited. Based on these accounts, he drew this beautiful and very detailed world map. It is currently under restoration, but its home is the Marciana library in the Piazza San Marco.

As you leave the vaporetto stop you glimpse the monastery and San Michele church. The cemetery stretches a long way and it can be difficult to see the other side of the island. The design gives the impression of garden rooms with walls, trees and paths dividing the area into compartments. There are numbered Catholic sections, Greek Orthodox, Protestant foreigners, soldiers and priests and nuns. Nowadays those laid to rest on San Michele have time limited stays of 20 or 50 years before their remains are moved to smaller wall crypts. Nothing is permanent.

There is an air of peace and quiet beauty on the island.

Among the moonlit marble lace,
That wreathes this avenue forlorn,
Some God has made his dwelling place
And takes his manna from the morn;
And every young and wandering soul,

That passes here, must pay its toll.

Far off the city fades away,
Save where one tow'r of rosy light,
Like some dissolving shaft of day,
Pierces the bosom of the night:
The distant lightning breaks its shroud:
Valhalla gleams beyond the cloud

Excerpt from Venice by Herbert Asquith

Momento di Mindfulness
Sacred Spaces

The whole visit will inevitably be a mindful experience. If you visit in the summer on an afternoon it will be quieter and you will have welcome shade and soft breezes from the lagoon.

Sad cypress, the monuments to those who have died. Mindfulness here needs no more than experiencing the island and a giving ourselves very simple reminder of the human need 'to live in the moment with gratitude'.

Stay Warm and See the City
If it is cold or raining then an afternoon on a Vaporetto is a good way to see the main sights of the city. There are reduced tickets for specific periods of time, for example, 3 days. These can be ordered on line and then picked up from a machine at some Vaporetto stations. For us, after settling in at the hotel, the walk to get the boat tickets is one of those 'rituals' which starts our holiday.

There are lots of different Vaporetto routes to choose from. The main ones are summarised here. You can go right out onto the edges of the lagoon, over to Punta Sabbioni or the islands. The service to Murano is excellent and you can go right through the canals of the island on the Number 3. A trip over to Lido is always worthwhile. The trip up the Canareggio Canal and then out via the port to the Giudecca Canal is different again.

The most popular are the boats which go up and down the Grand Canal. We always do this journey very early in the morning or late at night. Even in winter you can stand outside and watch the palazzos pass by and never tire of the view.

 Momento di Mindfulness
Navigating through & the Map of Mindfulness

Imagine going out from the port, out into the lagoon and then hitting the swell of the open Adriatic sea.

Sailing along, finding direction with only a basic map (with lots of missing information). Navigating by the stars in uncharted waters.

Imagine a Gale Force Storm.

Imagine being becalmed and making no headway for days and days.

Focus on your own life. Every day is a mental voyage, trying to flow along and not get caught up in the net of anxious thoughts. Navigating through different 'weather conditions'. Some sunny, calm days and other choppy, stormy days. 'Weather at sea analogies' fit very well with life experiences.

Navigating through life … Taking the helm. Wondering what the 'shipping forecast' might be for the next month or year. Think of mindfulness as a 'map' to guide you.

Via Vaporetto:

-Number 1 takes about 45 minutes to go the length of the Grand Canal and stops at every station along the way. It then continues out to the Lido.

160

-Number 2 is quicker, taking about 25 minutes to go up the Grand Canal, only stopping at the most popular stations of Tronchetto, Piazzale Roma, Ferrovia, San Marcuola, Rialto Bridge, San Toma, Accademia Bridge and San Marco. Number 2 also stops at Giudecca and only continues out to the Lido during the busy summer season.

-Number 3 is known as Murano line. From the Ferrovia (railway station) to Piazzale Roma (bus station) then five stops going round Murano.

-Numbers 4.1 and 4.2 go on a circular route around Venice. Number 4.1 runs in a clockwise direction while line 4.2 is anti- clockwise. From Murano the boat stops at San Michele, Fondamenta Nuove, Ferrovia, Piazzale Roma, Giudecca, San Zaccaria, and Fondamenta Nuove (again) before returning to Murano.

-Number 5.2 goes around Venice on the outside of the city, from Lido to Lido, passing through the Cannaregio Canal. The 5.2 goes clockwise and the 5.1 goes anticlockwise.

-Number 12 is the island express and goes from Fondamenta Nuova out to Murano, Burano, or Torcello.

-Number 14 leaves from San Zaccaria, makes a stop in Lido before heading out to Punta Sabbioni.

Momento di Mindfulness
Picturesque Venice - Photos as Keepsakes.

Last time we were in Venice I had the beginnings of an idea for writing this book. My starting point was to begin to take photos of places and scenes which seemed 'somehow mindful'. It might have been a canal view, crumbling brick work with trailing ivy. I took a photo of the roof of the loggia outside the Doges palace. I'd walked there many times but never looked up and noticed the ceiling and how the arches stretching ahead were perfect for a mindful contemplative moment.

Some of these photos will be posted on the website which compliments this book. The website is a way of showing some coloured illustrations of Venice which link with the themes of the book in a cost effective way. www.mindfulvenice.com is the accompanying web site. Further details at the end of the book.

By walking out with the aim of finding mindful scenes and taking a photo my walks through the city were different. I realised that taking a walk with a focused objective like this in mind made the walk a much more meditative experience. I also remembered my walks better afterwards. The photo of the grassy area at the base of La Scala Bovolo or looking out from the Riva degli Schiavoni to San Giorgio stand out. So this idea is here as a suggestion for a Mindful Moment.

Keeping a photo log of your vacation with a mindful theme strengthens and deepens memories. Memories are more likely to move into long term memory storage areas of the brain if we re-visit and re-call the details. Using a 'photo memory bank' practically in mindful meditational exercises when we return home makes the holiday experience more lasting. A 'memory bank' of snapshots leads to a stronger memory bank in the 'firing and wiring' and storage areas of our brains.

So when you go for a walk be on the lookout for 'photo opportunities'. Look for things which are different, quirky, thought provoking or things which inspire a feeling of calmness and peace.

When you find something to add to your photo log then give yourself a moment to pause while you stop and take the snap. Being on the lookout for different, maybe quirky things while you are out walking certainly adds depth and dimension to the walk. Make sure you have a memory bank of photos as a keepsake and to use practically when you return home.

Some ideas from my own seeing things differently photo 'memory bank':

Silvery shimmering water

Stone steps covered in algae and seaweed

Veiled views in the mist

Sun sparkling on the Zattere

Angels, cherubs, lions high above

A small terrier dog on a boat,

Damp and peeling walls

A bench in San Polo

The gold dome of San Marco

A well in a courtyard seen through an iron grid

Evergreen plants making an archway

Plague, Pestilence and Prayer

Venice was a place where plague resulted in more deaths than in most other cities in Europe. Between 1456 and 1528 there were fourteen outbreaks of plague. Venice's position on trade routes and its strong links with the East and Far East raised the odds of plague breaking out. Perhaps plague entered the city from fleas in a bolt of cloth. Merchants traded in silks and brocades.

The death toll in the plague of 1630 was at least a third of the city. The end of this outbreak led to Venetians creating the church of Santa Maria della Salute as an offering for deliverance from the epidemic.

Tiziano (or Titian) died of plague in August 1576. The artist who had given so much to the city in his life is one of the few citizens with a marked grave. Most victims were taken to plague houses on islands far out in the lagoon and then to mass graves on other islands. Tiziano was buried in the Basilica di Santa Maria Gloriosa dei Frari (the Friary).

In Medieval times death was ever present, whether in violent situations or in childbirth. 'In the midst of life we are in death' says the Anglican Book of Common Prayer. This is one of the few surviving features of the medieval approach to death in the 'offices of the dead.' What it tells us is that the living lived their lives with the closeness of death.
Both the Salute Church and the Church of the Redentore were built to give thanks for the end of a plague epidemic.

Chiesa del Santissimo Redentore
Tiziano died during the horrific plague of 1576. The Doge committed to building a church if the people of Venice were given salvation from the plague.

Palladio and Da Ponte made the Church of the Redentore rise up on the island of Giudecca. It is one of the finest examples of Palladian architecture. When the first foundations were laid, a temporary bridge of barges was made from the Zattere allowing the Doge to walk across to the site of the new church. Since that time there has been a repeat of this chain of boats across the Giudecca Canal. The Festa of the Redentore happens on the third Sunday in July. It's a time of celebration, fireworks and thanksgiving.

This spectacular church is a feature of the Venetian landscape.
The Chiesa del Santissimo Redentore has been embellished over the centuries by artists like Veronese and Tintoretto. Today on the eve of the Redentore the preparations begin at first light. Boats are decorated. As the sun sets the Bacino fills with these decorated boats. Then fantastic fireworks are let off from the island of San Giorgio with everyone in the city looking outwards and upwards for up to an hour. Some then go to sit out on the beach at the Lido and watch and wait for dawn – a sort of all-night vigil.

Then next day a bridge of barges is built connecting the island of Giudecca to the Zattere and the more religious aspects of the Feste begin. This is about redemption and thankfulness. The bones of the ancestors of many Venetians are still covering the islands where the dead were taken.

164

It was in the plague of 1630 that Charles de Lorme a French doctor developed what is often called 'the plague mask'. With its long beaked nose designed to prevent those in close contact with plague victims catching the disease. The beak was filled with preventative herbs. You will see this type of mask in shops and on posters around the city.

Church of Santa Maria Della Salute
The formation of the Church of Santa Maria Della Salute began in a council session after over a hundred thousand people had died. The vow was made that a church would be made to the glory of the Virgin Mary if the plague ended. It ended with cooler weather in the winter months.

An unknown architect called Longhena won the competition to envision and develop the Salute. His design was of an ambitious and tremendous octagonal church with inspiration from Venetian Baroque. His vision was for something "strange, worthy, and beautiful...in the shape of a round 'machine' such as had never been seen, or invented either in its whole or in part from any other church in the city."

The church was completed in 1682 more than fifty years later. It is a tremendously compelling building. It was also a feat of modern engineering, built of the Istrian stone which makes up much of Venice. The stones still rest on a foundation of 1,156,627 wooden pilings driven into the marshy, sandy ground. It contains pillars from a Roman Amphitheatre.

Look out for Titian, Tintoretto and Veronese in the Sacristy. It's possible to sit there quietly and gaze around the chapel. Look closely at the painting of the Feast of Cana. You can see a representation of Tintoretto at the wedding, dressed in pink, speaking to Veronese, while Mary whispers to Jesus, perhaps alerting him to the crisis around the wine.

The Festa della Salute happens on 21st November. A pontoon bridge is built across the Grand Canal to the Salute. People walk across the pontoon bridge to give thanks to Mary. Gondoliers take oars to receive a blessing from one of the priests who stands on the steps outside.

Visiting the Salute is a special experience. It has a very Eastern Orthodox style. It rises up on the lagoon landscape and is as impressive as the Doges Palace as you draw near to the city. It is surprising that it is often so quiet there. Perhaps because it is in Dorsoduro - though in fact by vaporetto it is actually very close to San Marco. It is a church to wander through and just experience and as individual inside as it is outside. We were lucky enough to catch a service of musical 'vespers' on 26th December one year. Magical, musical and spiritual place.

 Momento di Mindfulness
Being Kind to yourself

Jan Morris describes the Salute as 'a maiden aunt who looks beautiful tonight'. Someone giving us a reminder to be kind to ourselves and to others. The Salute and Redentore Churches are monuments to 'forgiveness' for deliverance from pain and death in the plague.

It isn't a concept we can easily identify with in the modern world. It is a very human emotion though to bargain with a deity. 'Dear Lord ... if only you would save a family member or friend from dying of a disease like cancer then I'll be faithful forever'. In Venice this bargaining with deities seemed to be a last resort and these two magnificent churches grew out of the promises.

Imagine a kind Great Aunt who is always 'in your corner' or 'on your side'. In mindfulness the concept of 'being kind to yourself' or self-compassion fits well here. Next time you are blaming yourself and sinking into the dismal swamp of despondency and lack of self-worth then imagine Great Aunt Salute saying something positive to boost your flagging spirits.

Places to Pause – small shrines
These churches were built for 'redemption' and hope for the future. On a smaller, quieter level Venice is filled with small shrines to the Virgin Mary. These are often inset into a wall in a calle or small calle. The small shrines often have a candle and flowers.

These are 'places to pause' which have most likely been here for centuries. Places where people paused and offered a small prayer to their local representation of the Madonna. Maybe a moment of fear for family wellbeing; maybe a moment of give thanks.

Plague and 'deliverance'   Deliver us from evil ...

Ancient and very human reactions and emotions to seek protection from adversity.

"The purest and most thoughtful minds are those which love colour the most."

John Ruskin, The Stones of Venice

Paint box palate - Ochre and Vermillion
Any Italian medieval city is a palette of colour. Buildings painted in terracotta, cream and yellow. Venice stands out because it has the luminous green canals and the open lagoon 'framing' the buildings.

Paints and pigments were limited in number until exploration and trade with the East began. In the 9th century traders brought back red vermillion which was derived from the ore cinnabar and this pigment was dangerously toxic. Red Vermillion gave a bright and permanent colour.

In the 12th-century, a new colour arrived in Venice from Afghanistan. This pigment was called ultramarine, meaning 'from overseas or beyond the sea'. This pigment was made from ground Lapis

Lazuli. giving a deep, vibrant shade. This pigment would play a huge role in the colour palette of Renaissance art.

So what colours would be in a palette of Venetian paints? I looked at some paint lists and charts. Here are three very different styles of names, yet all give a feeling of vibrant colours of Venice.

Traditional colours: yellow ochre, red ochre, green copper, umber, raw umber light, vermillion,

A modern twist: cavern clay, fireweed, turquish, gale force, armagnac, tantalizing teal, sunrise, restful, jute brown, polished mahogany

Roman inspired: muscat wine, cafe genoa, palazzo sand, vespasian stone, espresso nero, Apollo, sun, Tivoli, terracotta

 Momento di Mindfulness
Colourful & Individual Mantra

Choose your own list of paints. Read and imagine the colours from their wonderful sounding names. You can choose colours which appeal to you from the lists or search and find your own Venetian colour chart.

A combination of the names of paints on an artist's palate makes a good mantra. It links with visual images of the colours in art with colours of water, sky or architecture. Repeat this mantra to yourself for a few minutes. Imagine the colours at the same time as you say the words.

Mindful Murano
Murano is a mile out from Venice but seems like another world. The houses are colourful and a canal divides the houses. The island seems much closer to the lagoon, which is never far away from the houses. Murano Island was the home of glassmaking. The artisan glassmakers were restricted to the island due to the fire risk.

Where the lagoon meets the island you find the small glass factories. Most have a display and showroom for tourists. There are wooden landing stages for the guided tours. Jan Morris calls the glass making a "fine fiery mystery". In the days of the Republic it was a closely guarded secret and mystery. If a glassmaker left the city taking state secrets then they were inevitably tracked down and the assassin made sure the secrets of the trade were kept close to the island of glassmakers.

Murano glass is a soft glass which is famous for its quality, the beautiful array of colours, and the exceptional workmanship of the artisans on the island.

Glass has been made on the island of Murano since 1293. Venice is place where ancient techniques in glass making were developed and refined. Many modern techniques originated on Murano. My favourite is *Avventurina.* This is coloured glass that incorporates iridescent particles so the glass is never clear but has a design where the particles glint and shimmer. It might be gold, copper, chrome, or different metallic particles.

The technique of Avventurina has been used on Murano since the early 1600s. It is sometimes called '*pasta stellaria*', because of its star like quality. The stars catch the light and shine out from the glass.

Through a Glass Darkly
The earliest glass made in Venice looked rather like the round circular bottom of bottles. No longer open windows with shutters or opaque alabaster letting in minimal light but instead a covering of glass which lightened the room. These early glass windows were thicker than modern glass but still a wondrous improvement on what had gone before. These leaded glass windows make a great focus for mindfulness 'on the go'.

As you wander around the streets and in museums and buildings you will inevitably notice windows made with this individual glass. There are many colours, but the yellowy, ochre coloured are my favourite.

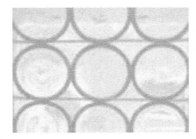

As you wander through the calles and palazzos of Venice look for examples of this traditional pattern of glass. Look at the pattern and the lead framed circles. Look through the glass at what you can see through the glass. It won't be a clear image as through a modern window but you will see shapes and patterns.

On the guided tours you will go on a walkway and see the artisans blowing the glass. You need to work at blanking out the people around you. Focus on the fire and the glassmaker as the glass shapes and colours develop. The workshop can be dark and the fire bright.

Often a hotel can organise a boat to a glassworks in Murano. Obviously this is a 'sales fuelled trip' with hopes of your buying an expensive chandelier but nevertheless it can be an option to consider.

Momento di Mindfulness
Anchor to La Serenissima

Find an inexpensive piece of Venetian Glass. Something which catches your eye. Hopefully something made in Venice, but you can never be sure of that nowadays. Nevertheless you will find something special which gives focus to the spirit of Venetian glass.

I have some miniature horses which were sold to us still warm from a basket on Murano. They have a lovely shades of light brown, ochre colour and shades of lighter and darker glass giving life to the prancing horses. After we had left the workshop and showroom an artisan came out with the basket and sold them to us. I know they are authentic as that glass was still warm and setting. One of those days in my childhood to treasure and remember.

I also have some tiny angel Christmas tree decorations in clear glass with gold tipped wings which I hang on the tree every Christmas.

And my final treasure are some green glass long drop ear rings. I bought these several years ago in a second hand shop in Dorsoduro. An elderly shopkeeper took them from the display and spent a lot of time and care wrapping them for me. I looked for the shop the next year and it was replaced by the all too frequent handbag shop.

Whatever you find then you can use it as a mindful moment to anchoring you to La Serenissima.

Sit at a table. Take your object of Venetian glass. Hold it. Feel it. Look closely at the form and qualities of the object. Its shape, colours, texture, size and weight. Put it in front of you on a table. Re-visit each

171

aspect again. Notice carefully. Does it have a purpose? Is it a paperweight, an ornament, a jug? How did it become glass? Made from grains of sand and elemental metallic particles. Practice active awareness as you notice the small details which would usually go unmissed.

Or alternatively do a search for an image of Vintage Venetian glass on the internet. Choose an image with colour and shape and focus on its colours and shape. Imagine the weight and texture of the object and continue with the exercise as above.

Dragons in Murano - San Donato and his Dragon

St George has a presence in Venice – with churches and even an island opposite San Marco. However there is another Dragon slayer in Venice and more specifically in Murano. Many of the Churches on Murano were lost during the Napoleonic and Austrian occupation. The church of the dragon slayer somehow survived. The Basilica dei Santi Maria Donato is a beautiful building with a circular apse with a layered balcony rising above it. Parts may date from the 7th century when the first refugees fled into the lagoon. The Eastern influence is obvious and you might be in Byzantium not Murano. It is one of the oldest and most fascinating churches in the Lagoon. The church faces the Canale San Donato. In the golden dome in the apse there is a 12th century glass mosaic of the Madonna standing out starkly from the gold leaf in its simplicity. This Madonna was created in the furnaces of Murano.

It is said the bones of the very dragon slain by San Donato of Arezzo are behind the altar. San Donato also lies within the church. Look carefully for signs of the dragon in the church.

There is a marble and mosaic floor, again Byzantine in style dating from 1141 around the same time as San Marco. The mosaics show a geometric pattern with peacocks and flowers embellished with precious stones. The similarities with San Marco are interesting. The bell tower is separate from the church. It's a simple but beautiful view as you walk towards the church.

Museo Vetraio di Murano

This is a collection of glass from Roman times through the 19th century. There are displays on the history of the craft on the island All in an individual, frescoed palazzo.

Mindful Mosaic

There is a variety of Venetian glass which is, in effect a tiny mosaic. I remember when I was a child that my mother had a bracelet made of several of these mosaics strung together. It was fascinating to look at the patterns. Probably hypnotic trance inducing!

Often the mosaics are a bright, vibrant colour with a patterned shape in the middle. The shape might be concentric circles, a star or a flower. They are quirky and never quite symmetrical. Unique and very Venetian. You can easily find bracelets, necklaces, key rings and paperweights made using these mosaics. I'm looking at a photo of a paperweight made of several mosaics now. It is easy to focus and become absorbed in the intricate kaleidoscope pattern.

Murano, Murrina and Millefiori

Mosaics have been made since ancient times. The Romans made mosaic for floors and wall coverings. The Venetian glassmakers reworked the technique making decorative mosaics in their own individual style.

Murrina is the technical term for the first step in making the mosaics. This involves making layered rods of glass. Different coloured layers are wrapped around each other.

The artisan then slices the tube to reveal a unique pattern. Repeated slices of the rod gives a recurrent blending pattern. One piece of the rod gives a startlingly simple design with a disk of glass with a distinct central pattern. The background disk can be any colour but is often

173

clear or dark blue. These individual mosaics are called
Millefiori. Millefiori is the technical term for these little mosaics and
means thousands of flowers.

Millefiori are set in metal and made into necklaces and earrings. I like
them in paperweights. There is something mindful about sitting at a
desk and staring at a paperweight. An individual mosaic can be chosen
and attention given to the pattern and the simple and beautiful effect.

 *Momento di Mindfulness*
Notice a unique pattern

Take a Venetian mosaic. If you can't find a mosaic then you can easily
search online and look at an image of a mosaic. You can focus your
attention on one individual mosaic or numerous mosaics in a joined
pattern.

Look at the mosaic. Focus on the pattern, the colours, the 'not quite
symmetrical' shape. Let your gaze go soft so the patterns merge.

Move into mosaic,
Millefiori, Millefiore,
Hear the word and its echo
Murano, Murrina, Millefiore,
See the pattern uniquely
Merging and melting
Moment for mosaic

Lighting the Way to Murano
If you travel to Venice from the airport by either water taxi or the
Alilaguna waterbus then you will pass Murano before you reach
Venice. The brick buildings stand out starkly against the lagoon. It's
canals are wider and it has the feel of being more open and less
crowded.

Murano is worth a dedicated visit during your stay. Return to the island
by vaporetto (and it's quite a good idea to go on a rainy day. Some of
the vaporetto go right through Murano, up the main canals and give you
quite a scenic tour.) Line 3 has 5 stops in Murano so you will see the
island from the boat. Lines 4.1, 4.2 and 12 also go out to Murano.

174

Far Faro Away

Murano has a working lighthouse. You can't visit it but you will know you are there because one of the Vaporetto stops is named after it – Faro. Built in 1912, the Murano Lighthouse is tall with a visual range of about 30 km.

Momento di Mindfulness
Lights Shining for Safety at Sea

As you pass by the Faro stop spend a moment considering the lighthouse and all the other lighthouses in the world, lights shining out for the safety of those at sea. Give a small moment of gratitude.

My grandfather was on the North Atlantic escort convoys in the Second World War and I come from a North Yorkshire seaside town with its small Cobble fishing boats. The sea is moody and dangerous. Even in the Venetian lagoon there can be peril for those at sea with sandbanks and the risk of going aground. The Faro is a symbol of safety and security.

Take a Ferry on Chillier Days

Ferry watching is an interest. It can become compulsive! There are regular small car ferries moving along the Zattere and out to the Lido. There are passenger ferries which stop at a terminus near San Zaccaria and also on Fundamenta Nuove, near the hospital. In the summer the ACTV ferries to Lido, Punta Sabbioni, Treporti and out to Burano will potentially be crowded and standing room only. At quieter times of the year travelling on one of the larger ferries can be a pleasant way to see the lagoon while keeping warm. There are times in mid-March when we've had the ferry almost to ourselves. If you travel to Lido and then Punta Sabbioni and ask politely to stay on for the return back to Venice they sometimes seem to allow this. Otherwise you have to get off and walk round the terminus and re-board again.

It makes sense to set off to the islands of the lagoon, especially Burano, in the early morning if you can manage the early rise. You will have a much more quiet and tranquil experience. The journey to Burano takes about 45 minutes.

In the winter the fog creeps over the lagoon and on market day you will still find Venetians taking the ferry from San Zaccaria to the Lido with shopping trolleys, returning bags brim full of fresh produce. In the Bacino you may even see a gondola close to the shore in the mist.

Venice is possibly the only place in Europe where the shopping trolley is an everyday necessity and they are used by all ages and not just an occasional elderly shopper. We should perhaps all learn from the Venetians and save our spines.

Momento di Mindfulness
Soaking Wet City - Different Perspective and Colour Scheme

A rainy day in Venice can be special. The first time I took my partner to Venice was on a rainy day in late May. It never stopped raining. We got very wet.

On a rainy day the paving stones glisten. The calles give some element of protection. The raindrops can cause ripples on the surface of the canals. I have to say that it is even more special if the sun comes out and shines through the raindrops.

Seeing the contrast between the colours of a cloudy city and a sun filled city is special. In the cloudy colour palette the winter whites, russet and dark browns stand out. In a sunny palette the yellows, golden ochres and terracotta take over. The colour of the water changes too - grey to turquoise is possible in a very short space of time.

Part 9

LATE AFTERNOON TEATIME

"There is something so different in Venice from any other place in the world, that you leave at once all accustomed habits and everyday sights to enter an enchanted garden."

Mary Shelley

Welling Up (Literally)

Every campo seems to have a well. A beautiful well, made of Istrian stone, sometimes with a sculpted pattern and sometimes in plainer stone.

Its intriguing to learn that early Venetian city planning developed this wonderful network of campos and campielli out of the practical necessity to collect a supply of water.

The marshy lagoon landscape has no fresh water. It isn't possible to sink a well to draw water from a water table. Those early Venetian engineering minds decided the only option was to collect and filter rainwater. To do this they needed a large surface area to collect the rainwater and funnel it down into underground storage. Hence the campos spread throughout the city.

This is also why you only see wells in campos or in the inner courtyards of palazzos. As you walk through the streets you will catch sight of inner courtyards with a well in the centre. Under each well is a collection area or cistern.

In the middle of the campos are cisterns which are around 6 metres deep. Each was filled with river sand surrounded by a layer of thick waterproof clay which acted as a barrier against the saltwater. The water was purified as it passed through the sand. These campo were designed with guttering to drain rainwater into the well. The campos were not flat and with lower levels around each gutter. The rain filtered down through the sand to the waterproof clay bottom and then filled up the well. Welling up – literally. The water could then be drawn up with buckets.

I've read that wells could be used only twice per day, (morning and in the evening) at the ringing of the "wells bells".

There came a point in the seventeenth century where the water supply needed supplementing. Fresh water began to be brought by boat from the River Brenta. The boats were filled with water and rowed back to Venice to fill up the wells from wooden pipes. The boatmen were called "acquaroli". Their role expanded over time because they began to collect the rubbish (garbage). Water and rubbish were kept very separate so the water remained pure.

178

In 1881 work started in laying an iron pipe under the lagoon to bring river water to the city. It took 3 years to build and was celebrated with the construction of a fountain in the middle of Piazza San Marco.

Momento di Mindfulness
Acqua Engineers

Find a well in a campo or courtyard. Spend a few minutes focusing on the stonework, any design or pattern of the well. Touch the stone and feel the texture and temperature. If you have a water spray in your bag then take it out and spray your face and hands with water.

Notice the paving on the floor and the guttering facilitating the drainage of rainwater into cistern storage below the well.

Give thanks for human ingenuity in engineering design. The ability to find solutions to necessities like a safe, clean water supply.

A quick mindful travel aside about a water spray. These are invaluable and readily available at farmacias across the city. Or you can take a plastic spray bottle and fill it with bottled or tap water. If you feel tired it is refreshing. If your feet are tired then it can be a quick way of reviving them. Each time you use the water spray then make it an opportunity to breathe in, breathe out and take a moment out. A small size water spray is invaluable in airport lounges and on the runway while waiting to take off.

Glasshouse in Giardini

Serra dei Giardini is a relatively recent addition to the landscape. The original greenhouse dates from 1894 but it has a complicated history which resulted in it becoming almost derelict until the early part of the 21st century. The greenhouse was built of glass and ironwork to create a "tepidarium" for palm trees and other plants at the Biennale.

It is now a quiet glasshouse cafe which is away from the crowds and gives a warm haven on a colder autumn or winter day. There is a flower shop, coffee shop and sometimes musical and art events. The entrance is part way along Via Garibaldi.

Momento di Mindfulness
Toast & Tea

Pause for tea and perhaps a toasted sandwich (un toast) or thick hot chocolate. Enjoy the humid warmth on a cooler day. Enjoy the way the sun's rays are magnified and warm the glasshouse. Give attention to what you can see in and around this special quiet haven for tired feet.

This place was newly built as an exhibition piece but then decayed over time till it was almost derelict. Now it is having this renaissance. Live in the moment and enjoy a quiet 'moment meditivato' in the Giardini Glasshouse.

Arsenale – Engineering Ingenuity

Visiting the area around the Arsenale in the late afternoon or early evening in summer works well. The sun's strength is fading and whether you walk or take a vaporetto to the Arsenale stop the crowds should be thinning. On reflection I don't think we have ever specifically planned to visit Arsenale at this time of day – we've just ended up here.

Often after a long walk across the city from Rialto, through Campo Santa Maria Formosa and on to the café and restaurant near the Arsenale entrance. Even on a warm day in March it's possible to have an early evening meal of pizza or a bowl of pasta washed down with the slightly fizzy red house wine. It's possible to walk around this quiet area and get an idea of the enormity of the ship building history of this place.

Ships needed to be built in Venice from the start of the first settlements in the lagoon. The Arsenale Nuovo was ship building on a large scale and evolved into the most efficient workshop in Europe. The great galley ships began to take form. The galley was different because its frame was built first. Less timber was needed than for ships whose hulls were built first. With organisation the time it took to build a ship reduced significantly. This was a factory production line approach. Artisans working in sequence on a small part of the ship building process.

In the 16th century Arsenale was the most efficient shipbuilding workshop the world had ever seen. It went further than ship building, the ships were fully kitted out with sails, supplies, rope and munitions. A galley a day was built in the Arsenale - it seems hard to comprehend this. I've watched gullets being built in Turkey and the time spent on craftsmanship is intense and takes many months. How a seaworthy galley could be built in a day is remarkable. More understandable after I read that in 1593 Galileo was an adviser to the Arsenale, helping to solve problems and devising some of the innovations in the production line. Each artisan had a small piece of the sequential process and this was a highly skilled operation.

Nowadays the Arsenale is a quiet and interesting place to visit and see a different aspect of Venice. There is a cafe/restaurant near the entrance where you can spend a quiet time. Lions guard the gates and are covered in what has turned out to be runic symbols. The Biennale takes over some of the buildings and there is a Naval museum. It is worthwhile visiting these as you can as you will be able to see more of the Arsenale. The vaporetto no longer goes through the Arsenale due to security restrictions as it is a functional Navy base. There is great excitement in one of the Donna Leon novels when the pilot radios to ask for permission to go through the Arsenale and Brunetti is excited to travel through this now hidden waterway.

If you watch the movie The Tourist then Arsenale is the centre of the British Secret Service where Angelina Jolie one of the secret agents reports in.

There is even a reference to the Arsenale in Dante's inferno:

> *Boils in winter the tenacious pitch*
> *To smear their unsound vessels over again*
> *For sail they cannot; and instead thereof*
> *One makes his vessel new, and one recaulks*
> *The ribs of that which many a voyage has made*
> *One hammers at the prow, one at the stern*
> *This one makes oars and that one cordage twists*
> *Another mends the mainsail and the mizzen...*

Runic inscriptions - a mystery solved

The marble lions at the gate of the Arsenale and their backs are covered with Runes. They are thought to be booty brought back from Athens. For centuries no one knew what the strange inscriptions were. Then a Danish Scholar identified them as Norse (Viking) Runes. These were carved on the lion in the eleventh century by order of Harold the Tall. Harold the Tall, also known as Harold Hardrada, died in the invasion of England in 1066. He dies at the Battle of Stamford Bridge in the north of England just prior to the Battle of Hastings.

Momento di Mindfulness
A Wonder of the World

Stand somewhere near the Arsenale Vaporetto stop. Face the lagoon and the waters of the Bacino.

It's good if it's a sunny day but one of the wonderful things about Venice is its unique weather. Even when the weather forecast says there is a low chance of sun there is often an hour or a half hour when the sun shines through. It doesn't matter though because the silvery grey clouds, the mist or heat haze all give a different view.

Feel the air, the breeze in the spring, the hot heat of an August day. Connect. Make your eyes go hazy as you gaze across towards the Isle of San Georgio. If there were 'Seven Views of the World' this would be one of them. It's a scene to savour. You will have seen it in books, movies and paintings.

Feel connected with the scene. Close your eyes very briefly and still see the scene in your mind. Open your eyes again and merge the scene you had in your mind while your eyes were closed with what you see now. Notice any subtle changes, like a boat moving or a vaporetto coming into the scene.

You will want to remember this scene forever. Here you are in a special moment in your life. Experience and savour it fully.

You can close your eyes and open them again and repeat this 'mindful moment' if you want or leave it at this point.

Now take out your phone or camera and take a photo. Snapshot the view and make the memory of this moment stronger.

There are some benches along the Riva near the bridge which goes over towards the Via Garibaldi and the Giardino boat stop. If you are lucky enough to find one free on a sunny day (probably out of season) then seize the moment and sit. Sit and stare at the Bacino and the wider lagoon. For me it is like watching an ongoing movie. I can get lost in watching the water, backwash from boats, the noise of the low geared vaporettos and feel the sea breeze around me. Take a moment and be part of this unique 'mindful moment' movie.

Sant'Elena

Sant'Elena is an island to the eastern edge of the city and is part of Castello. It was originally an island with its church and monastery. Now Sant'Elena is joined to Venice by three bridges. It's a green space with a park and the Football Stadium and is the home of the Biennale.

If you have time then take a 'mindful green walk' through this area of the city. It is a part of the city which gives an impression of how it would have been in other parts of the city centuries before at the time when land was being reclaimed from the Lagoon. The days when some of the campos were green grazing areas and meadows.

Momento di Mindfulness
A Mindful Walk through Green Spaces

Walk the boundaries of the area and notice the green spaces throughout Sant' Elena. This area is the outside of edge of Venice. Experience the quiet and serenity of the locality.

Maybe reflect on the mindfulness of soccer/football. There is focus and shared purpose in the teamwork. Those who are watching can become almost trance like in their absorption in the game.

Archivo & Biblioteca

Many years ago my parents took my brother and I to look at the State Archive of Venice, which at that time was open to tourists. In those days tourists rarely found the area of San Polo and we set off using a map to find our way from Rialto to the Archives next to the Frari. This would have been the early 1980s.

I remember a place with wide shelves piled high with books, scrolls and maps. Ancient documents wherever I looked. The memory of this

184

visit has always stayed with me. My partner and I went back 5 years ago and very soon realised that the Archive is now only open to academic scholars. This is probably a sensible decision, but I'm still glad I had the experience of seeing this treasure trove.

It is still possible to get 'in touch' with ancient documents and books. Visit the Biblioteca Marciano. This was specially designed and built by Jacopo Sansovino as home to the Greek and Latin manuscripts given to the Republic in 1468 by Cardinal Bessarion. The collection includes an incredibly special manuscript of the Iliad dating from the 5th or 6th century and the map of the world collated in Venice by the monk Fra Mauro.

During the construction Sansovino was arrested because part the ceiling of the new palace collapsed. He was released after he paid the expenses for the damage.

The building itself is small but delightful. The lobby has a ceiling painted by Titian aptly called "La Sapienza" ("knowledge"). On the ceiling of the hall are twenty-one portraits, by seven artists chosen by Titian and Sansovino. Three of the best known are by Veronese. On the walls of the hall are portraits of philosophers by Tintoretto and Veronese.

Momento di Mindfulness
Past Times

While you are walking focus and spend 5 minutes imagining the city as it was in the past. Perhaps the days when artists were carrying their tools to a local Scuole or Church to do a day's work creating a fresco. Perhaps the dark days of occupation after 1943 and the years of hunger and deprivation after the second world war. The city has been occupied by Napoleon, the Austrians and the Nazi regimes. Occupation tends to develop that unique, independent and 'partisan' character.

I hesitate to suggest you imagine the days of plague and pestilence, when those plague masks really were worn with a protective purpose. Or the courtesans calling to customers in the decadent days of the later Republic.

I'm lucky enough to have memories of Venice from the early 1970s onwards and can wind back time and imagine a more recent period of time

San Giorgio - Views from a Campanile

The view from the top of the Campanile on San Giorgio is said to be the best view in Venice. This Campanile was built in 1791 after the previous one collapsed. The tower rises 60 metres high. Take the elevator/lift up and get a clear view of St Marks and the Doges Palace, a view which you don't get from the Campanile in the Piazza. There are no queues waiting to go up this Campanile.

The first records of the island date back to 790, when a church was built on what was known as the 'Island of the Cypresses'.

An earthquake in 1223 destroyed the original monastery buildings. San Giorgio remained a Benedictine monastery until the early 19th century when Napoleon made it a military zone. An artillery store was built plus a military dock with two watch towers, which can be seen from Riva degli Schiavoni.

Count Vittorio Cini bought the island in 1951 and became a 'super hero' of restoration. The monastery was pretty much ruined after the years of military occupation. Cini had the aim of restoring the island, creating an internationally renowned cultural foundation with a key role in Venetian life. The Foundation is dedicated to the Arts. Programmes cover art history, Venetian history, music (especially Vivaldi) and drama. The Foundation continues the work today and more projects keep being added.

There have been several churches on the site. This church is a famous design by Palladio who stayed on San Giorgio for twenty years. The church has Tintoretto's 'Ultima Cena' (The Last Supper) and 'Raccolta della Manna' (The Fall Of Manna). There is a wooden carving showing scenes from the life of Saint Benedictus.

The monastery is completely restored with amazing care for detail and choice of materials. The refectory was designed by Palladio and restored by the Foundation is particularly impressive. There are guided tours of the monastery starting at 10.00 – 17.00 hrs. The tour showcases three gardens. One garden has 4 cypress trees which echoes back to the ancient name 'Island of Cypresses'. The cloisters, which were created by Palladio. And finally the Borges knot garden which was designed in 2011. The Borges Garden design combines a traditional herbal knot garden pattern with aspects of contemporary design.

186

The Borges garden is based on a story by Argentine writer Jorge Luis Borges, an Argentinian writer called The Garden of Forking Paths. It is refreshing and calming in its symmetry.

If you walk along the path, towards the other side of the island you will find a glass museum. It's a small museum with no entry charge and worth visiting.

With the commitment, time and funding given to San Giorgio by the Cini Foundation this restoration has made the monastery and island very special indeed. The island is now the perfect, quiet place to spend a time and gaze across to San Marco.

Momento di Mindfulness
An Impression of Venice

This is the place to take your holiday snap of Piazza San Marco. If you go up the Campanile it may be your holiday snap is an aerial view of Venice. Or it may be you walk to the edge of the island to the vaporetto stop and take a photo from there. San Giorgio is a perfect place to take your holiday snap.

Venice's Accademia della Belle Arte
This is likely to be an early evening or early morning visit. At other times of the day it is going to be busy. There are many guides and sites packed with information about the Accademia. It's world famous like the Uffizi in Florence. This gallery space is filled with masterpieces of Venetian art up to the nineteenth century. You can follow a progressive timeline with some thematic exhibitions.

The Accademia opened in Dorsoduro in 1750 and was housed in one of the historic Scuola buildings. The buildings of the Scuola della Carità and the de-consecrated church of Santa Maria della Carità are utilised by the gallery. The Accademia was one of the first places in Europe to teach the skills of art restoration and still offers courses today.

Venice is alive with art. The system of Scuole and sponsorship gave rise to a tradition of painting which lasted for centuries and still links with the Biennale today. Every church seems to have frescoes or paintings which are significant in art history. However, as in Florence, the faces of the people in the paintings were often based on the people of the time. People who were living and walking around the city at the time of the painting. The faces of real people. In the Frari there is an image of Titians' wife, which is poignant as soon after she died in childbirth.

Carpaccio often gives insight into daily life inside a Palazzo. People in his paintings might be sitting, working, talking or helping with preparations for childbirth. There are also animals in art, the pets living alongside people at the time of the paintings. Sometimes on the street I see a face and think I recognize the person but it is more likely a resemblance to the faces I've seen on paintings around the city. The link with history in Venice is very strong.

Momento di Mindfulness
People and Paintings / Locals and Life

Consider for a moment the connections art gives us to people of the past. Focus on a face or faces in a painting and imagine what they are saying and how their life might be in Medieval Venice, with the fragility of life and the threat of death in childbirth or plague never far from daily reality.

Modern Twists

Biennale
The Biennale began in 1895 with its centre in the Giardini gardens. It is biennial - hence the name. It runs from May to November. Today the pavilions are permanent structures ready for contemporary art exhibitions. There is an international atmosphere with various countries taking pavilions all linking to a central theme. In 2019 the theme of *May You Live In Interesting Times.* A previous theme was *Things not always what they seem.* The Film Festival is part of the Biennale and there is a developing Contemporary Dance festival in the spring.

The model of the original Biennale persists to this day in the City of Culture Model in Europe. Take an area which is in need of investment and give it a vibrant cultural focus.

There are fringe events throughout the city and these are often free to enter. This gives an opportunity to go inside amazing palazzos which would not usually be open to the public. Experiencing medieval Gothic interiors and catching glimpses of canals and rooftops through windows or terraces.

The Guggenheim - often simply called "Peggy's'.
Peggy Guggenheim lived on the Grand Canal in the Palazzo Venier dei Leoni. Peggy collected contemporary art and promoted the work of emerging artists of the time like Jackson Pollock. Now the collection includes twentieth century themes of Cubism, Futurism, Metaphysical, Abstract expressionism, Surrealism. Sometimes there are temporary themed exhibitions. There are works by Dali, Picasso, Ernst, Mondrian and Kandinsky. The sculpture garden is a tranquil retreat from the busy city. The garden and cafe have views out onto the Grand Canal.

'Peggy's' opens late, closing at 18:00 hrs. so it's a perfect visit at the end of a busy day.

Momento di Mindfulness
One Piece of Art

Use the technique of visiting a gallery or museum and wandering around mindfully with your focus on finding one piece of art which really appeals to you. Maybe it's a painting, or part of a painting or a sculpture. Something with a modern pattern or effect. Give focused attention to the specific details of this one piece of art. Gaze at absorb the details and commit to your vacation 'memory bank'. This is another holiday souvenir to take home with you.

Shaded Places in the late afternoon.
After a day of walking and exploring you will inevitably have tired legs. It's the time of day to find a place to sit and watch the world go by. I try to go to the Zattere if the weather is sunny. It isn't a campo but this promenade along the waterfront is my end of day treat, sometimes with a Prosecco or Lemon Soda depending on my mood. Finding a seat at a cafe or on a bench in a campo and just looking around me and paying attention to what is going on.

One campo which is worth visiting at this time of day is San Giacomo dall' Orio. This campo is in Santa Croce but is also close to San Polo and Dorsoduro. In the early evening, you'll find people sitting with a Spritz talking, people out walking, greeting family and acquaintances and children playing together in the campo. This campo is well shaded by plane and locust trees and this gives welcome shade in the heat of summer. There are benches all around to sit in the shade and muse on the scene. Then hopefully you will hear the San Giacomo bells ring out, creating a special evening atmosphere.

San Giacomo has been called one of the most beautiful churches in Venice and is also one of the oldest dating from around 976 AD. It's a small church with an intricate wooden ceiling and an assortment of Byzantine treasures

Momento di Mindfulness
Contrasting Fast & Slow Thinking

It's been a long day of walking and exploring. Walking slow or fast at times. Maybe even coming to a halt in a queue or in the crush of people on a ferry. Contrasting moments in a day in Venice.

Now contrast fast and slow thinking. Review your day of exploring Venice mindfully at speed with 'fast thinking'. The spool of memory film winding at a fast rate. Next review the same day but this time with slow motion thinking. Slow the speed down and notice more details of the day.

Cats & Dogs - the Venetian Way

I can spend hours watching dogs out and about 'sniffing the air'. The Venetian dogs seem to take the Passagiata or daily promenade very seriously! They proudly walk alongside their owners, greeting their canine friends. Increasingly the modern Venetian dog is small in size and has been to a boutique for a coat and matching collar. The shops selling accessories for pets are quite noticeable - you will see at least one as you walk around the city.

I've wondered recently about Venetian cats. As a child I remember seeing a lot of cats and that's no longer the case. Maybe they are house cats now or keep to the quieter parts of the city. Maybe it is just a trend for dogs and not cats at this point in the 21st century.

A Prosecco & some Chiccetti in the late afternoon

Once in late December we were waiting for a late flight home. We passed the Osteria Dell Squero close to San Trovaso and it was quiet inside with places to sit, which was unusual. We went in and had one of the most special times as dusk drew in and it grew gradually colder outside.

We drank glasses of Prosecco and had an assortment of the small Cicchetti, choosing from the plentiful glass case on the counter. The Osteria had small sandwiches, crostini slices with a range of salame, salty cheese, San Danielle ham, pancetta, radicchio, zucchini, olives, aubergines, walnuts, artichoke, chilli, cuttlefish and tuna.

This was possibly the first place that we had Prosecco in Venice. Al Squero was discovered by our daughter who was in Venice on a shoestring budget and the Osteria certainly is excellent value for money. In the summer you will find people drinking prosecco in disposable glasses by the side of the canal.

The view is of a boat building yard or Squero. Boats are repaired and gondolas may be built. It is an ancient craft and a connection to the past.

This has become one of our special places in Venice. The hotel I've discovered and grown to love is close by. The Zattere is a few footsteps away. I've been to Florian's and enjoyed it, but I shall return to the Osteria Squero again and again. It's got special memories. And however busy it is, even in the height of summer we've always been made to feel very welcome.

191

Further up this same canal is Cantinone–già Schiavi. This is a lovely, historical wine shop and Bacaro. The Cicchetti are definitely worth trying. Brunetti visits this Cantinone in one of the Donna Leon novels. There is a vast assortment of bottles of wine available. There are also many wines which you can buy by the 'ombre' sized glass to drink along with your Cicchetti or Crostini.

 *Momento di Mindfulness*
Grace of Gondolas

One of the iconic symbols of Venice has to be the Gondola. While writing this book I was acutely aware that not everyone will be able to afford a ride in a Gondola. The Gondola has a flat bottom and a unique style of rowing with one oar. The strength and skilled knowledge of water levels, tides, tight corners is incomparable. For many centuries the gondola was the main form of transport in the city. The larger Traghetti still cross the Grand Canal at various points.

The Gondolas move through the canals in a quiet and confident way. There is a grace to gondolas which is unique. Sometimes at the Squero

Boatyard you will see a gondola there to be repaired. Some years ago we saw one of the rare historic gondolas with an ornate, enclosed cabin which was there to be repaired.

Watch a Gondola moving through a canal. Focus on the design and then the oar and how the gondolier deftly propels the gondola through the canals.

If you do have opportunity for a gondola ride then you will see canals it is impossible to see by foot. Some of the canals have no footpath alongside and you would travel along these smaller canals.

San Trovarso in Advent
The Church of San Trovarso is near to the Squero boat yard and the Cicchetti & Prosecco Bars. We've been lucky enough to spend Christmas in Venice and it was an incredibly special experience. The church of San Trovarso had a notice on its door about concerts on all the Sundays in Advent. We've been to two of these now. It's an incredibly special and very local experience. The music is of high quality. It seems to be organised by the organ scholar at the church and features other guest musicians. Local people wander in and take seats and the music starts. Everyone listens. Occasionally someone will stand up or come in and often with a shopping bag. Then at the end there is a standing ovation. You very much feel part of a community.

The San Trovarso Church dates back to 1028 and rebuilt in 1548. In the chancel are two paintings, *Adoration of the Magi* and *Expulsion of Joachim from the Temple* (before 1587) by Tintoretto. There is a

193

copy of The Last Supper by Tintoretto with the original now in the National Gallery in London. The Church was on the border between the areas of two local families in conflict. It is said the double facade of the church is so that the two families would not have needed to meet when coming in or leaving the church for a service. The feud is well documented in early Venetian history - so who knows if the church has two entrances for this reason - it's plausible.

The Church is a lovely neighbourhood church on a canal near the Zattere and if you happen to be in Venice on an Advent Sunday in the early evening you may find a rather special concert for the cost of a donation to the church.

Walking and Learning
La Bussola Association actually offers free walking tours of the city. Of course, the guide is giving their time and there is an expectation of a donation for the information and insight into the city.

'Members of our association take care in promoting the city's museums and churches, not just the main landmarks, but also other unique hidden gems that Venice is so rich with. There are over 100 churches and 40 museums in this little town, and each one of them is packed with art.'

The goal is to signpost tourists to famous and less well known landmarks, giving cultural insights to visitors. The website gives an outline of the tours and showcases 'wooden ceilings in Venice' and 'quirky palazzos'.

Miss Garnet's Angel - a Venetian Miss Marple

About twenty years ago we went to Venice for New Year with my parents. My Mum had just finished reading a book called 'Miss Garnet's Angel' by Salley Vickers. Our holiday became a little focused on the book and we set out to find the church with the carving of the dog and the boy with a fish. My daughter who was about 8 years old at the time became interested in churches and carved stone in a way she never had been before. I learnt that you can encourage a child's natural interest in a place by linking it with stories. Clearly the complexities of the Garnet story were beyond a small child but she had a definite interest in the character and the church.

After a lot of searching through calles we did find the Church of the Angel Rafael in Dorsoduro. I'm not sure but I think we were almost at the back of the island and the port of San Basilio. It was a lovely small campiello on a sunny day in January. The Church was closed but we found the carved plaque on the side. We had lunch at the Osteria next to the Church and it was a very traditional Venetian stew with bay leaf - certainly not the usual Menu Turistica. Some years later I returned and went into the church and looked at the art and architecture. Inside the Chiesa dell' Angelo Raffaele is the series of paintings by Guardi telling the story of Tobias (the book of Tobit).

Sometimes there are transition points in life and Miss Garnet, a retired teacher was experiencing one of these times. A grief in the death of a friend and an unexpected legacy. A courageous decision to travel to Venice to love there in an apartment during the winter months. Miss Garnet becomes immersed in the beauty, the art and the ex-pat community. She even begins to develop feelings for an art dealer which is a totally new experience in her life. Linked to this is the story of twins who are restoring a 14th century chapel. There is a mystery and Miss Marple aspect when a valuable painting of an angel goes missing from the chapel along with one of the twins. The twin is called Toby and the parallel story has a Tobias. Also linked is the story of an ancient tale of Tobias and the Angel and Garnet discovers panels in the local church relating to this story.

This is a multi-layered, mysteriously haunting novel which takes apart reality and puts it back together with different perspectives. The tale of Tobias, who goes on a journey to Medea, unaware he is accompanied by the Archangel Raphael is interwoven with Miss Garnet's contemporary journey. Venice is the backdrop to Miss Garnet 'discovering herself' and searching out change. This is an insight into a different Venice with roots in the past and where past and present seem to merge together. Miss Garnet feels the spirit of the Angel Raphael.

As I walk towards the Church I almost expect to see Miss Garnet coming round the corner.

This ancient tale within the Chiesa dell' Angelo Raffaele, told by the series of paintings by the elder Guardi of Tobias who travels to Media unaware he accompanied by the Archangel Raphael became the story which underpins Miss Garnet's Angel.

 Momento di Mindfulness
Patterns & Reflections

Shade from the sun becomes important in the summer months. Notice the contrast and whether you are walking in sunshine or shade. Notice the differences in temperature and light levels. Look out for shadows of people and buildings as you walk along.

Look for the patterns of sunlight and shade on the walls and pavements.

Look for reflections of buildings in the water.

Next imagine someone has spilled a gigantic tube of glitter all over the city. The Palazzos and Canals are covered in glimmering specks of gold and silver.

Notice any sparkles and glitter on the palazzos and canal. Notice and notice again. If you look carefully you will notice sparkles, even on a dull and damp day.

Byzantium & the Orient
Even today these names still sound just a little exotic. It was in the East in Byzantium that Venetians discovered mosaic patterns and returned to the city to add the designs to their churches. The merchant adventurers found precious stones and gold which glimmered and glistened in the dull European winters.

San Marco Cathedral was embellished and decorated with jewelled treasures from Eastern countries.

Oriental spices and silks which were discovered and brought back to the city. The city was enriched by this trade in precious stones, silk and spices. Venice was the main trading post between Europe and the East.

Momento di Mindfulness
Patterns - Tiles, Marble and Arabesque

Choose a tile or a piece of marble somewhere during your walk. Focus fully on the pattern and design. Appreciate the pattern. Close your eyes and try to still see the pattern as a picture in your head.

If the tile or marble is in a building then touch and feel the temperature. If it is ceramic or marble does it feel cool to the touch.

Continuing Patterns - unbroken Arabesque
Look out for 'Arabesque'. This is a very specific pattern which is both continuous and repetitive. It's a design often found decorating walls and plasterwork in Venice. It is linear with patterns like scrolling, winding foliage or curving lines. The same simple pattern is repeated many times.

Many Arabesque patterns in Western Europe are influenced by Islamic art. Others have their roots in ancient Roman, Greek or Lycian (ancient Turkish) patterns. Designs from Byzantium and the Far East permeate every aspect of Venetian architecture.

These flowing unbroken Arabesque patterns can be seen throughout the city. Look out for them and make your own collection. Take photos when you see an Arabesque design.

Step aside and consider life and living as a flowing pattern with continuous winding lines and patterns.

Marco Polo

Marco Polo was born in 1254. His father had been absent most of his life and returned to Venice when Marco was about fifteen. Then when his father and uncle set of on another voyage the young Marco accompanied them. He was a 'merchant of Venice' and explorer of the world. The older Polos had already met Kublai Khan and Marco became close to the Emperor in his palace in Xanadu. The Polos became emissaries for the Emperor and Marco was even a travelling tax collector and 'special envoy' in China and South East Asia. The Polos were away for 24 years.

In 1298, three years after his return to Venice, Marco was captured after leading a galley into battle against rival state of Genoa. While in prison he met fellow prisoner Rustichello of Pisa who was already a writer of medieval romantic stories. Polo told the saga of his adventures and Rustichello recorded these into a manuscript. This may have been the first documented ghostwriter!

They were set free in 1299, with a completed book and soon after Marco Polo became a famous name. *'Livre des merveilles du monde' (Book of the Marvels of the World)* and more commonly known in English translation as *The Travels of Marco Polo*

Polo describes amazing creatures and we now know these as crocodiles, monkeys, elephants and rhinoceroses. Crocodiles are giant, sharp-clawed "serpents" that could "swallow a man … at one time." Not unsurprisingly Polo thought the rhinoceros were unicorns. New geographical places like China opened up to readers.

Polo became a wealthy merchant, got married and had 3 children. He was buried in the church of San Lorenzo in 1324. He was certainly not the first European to visit China. However because of the chance meeting with Rusticello the chronicles of his travels and experience gave a record of his adventures. Fra Mauro's famous map was partly inspired by Marco Polo.

Over time people started to question the validity of his tales. Were some of them lies? Rusticello the romantic author certainly placed Polo in heroic roles to add court intrigue and adventure to the saga. On his deathbed he is reported to have said "I did not tell half of what I saw."

I always thought that the voyage somehow opened up trade routes, but it seems the window closed for travels to that specific part of the Silk Road with death of Kublai Khan around the time the polo family returned to Venice.

Momento di Mindfulness
Collaborative Communication – networking with others

Marco Polo's family were clearly 'out there' developing a connecting gateway between Europe and the Orient. Marco Polo seems to have had diplomatic skills at an early age. He must have had to become a tax collector and envoy for Kublai Khan.

Connections and networking are the basis of so much successful human communication. Collaborative communication rather than competitive positioning and conflict.

Maybe put the spirit of this approach into practice today and have a conversation with someone you haven't talked with before at the hotel where you are staying.

Or spend some time considering how you might strengthen your network of friends and family at home. Strengthening your own supportive, collaborative communication with others.

Sometimes it's helpful to draw a simple mind map of your supportive network of family and friends. Once you have this on paper you can then reflect with gratitude for the special people in your life.

Positive psychology research tells us that when we let someone know how much we appreciate them and actually write and thank them for this it not only makes them feel better but it makes us feel more positive too. Go retro and send someone a postcard but make sure you include a sentence about how you value them. Or if locating a stamp (*un francobollo* in Italian) for a postcard is just too much to think about while on vacation then send someone an photo from your holiday by email or messenger app including a similar message about how you are thankful they are in your life.

Part 10

SUNSET

"When I seek another word for 'music',

I never find any other word than 'Venice'."

Friedrich Nietzsche

Call at a Campo

At some point, as you wander through Venice you will walk along a narrow calle which suddenly and unexpectedly opens out into the wide open space of a campo. These campos are places of community where families gather and you will see friends greeting each other and sharing news. You may see children playing football. A campo is the vibrant heart of the neighbourhood.

If you want to then you will find much more information on each campo in guidebooks or online features. Here there is a focus on just taking a mindful stroll through the campo with the spotlight on a few key characteristics. The campo covered in *Exploring Venice Mindfully* are:

Santa Margarita, Santo Stefano, San Polo, Campo Ghetto, Santa Maria Formosa, San Giovanni e Paulo, San Barnaba and Via Garibaldi (which for me is an honorary campo).

Campo Santa Margarita

We must have just missed finding Margarita so many times over the years. It is actually a very large campo so how we missed it is incredible and says something about the winding streets of Venice. The first time we found it was after a visit to Miss Garnet's Church of the Angel Rafael. It was a bright, sunny, winter's day and we emerged in a campo where local people were gathered and children were playing football. We braved sitting at an outside table in the winter sunshine and were delighted when sparrows came to take crumbs. (aware that some of you may not like this to happen for you but for us it was quite special). That was back in 1998.

In recent years the proximity to the university has made this a vibrant area with bars staying open later than in most other parts of the city. It's a good place to sit and watch the world go by while sipping an Aperol spritz or negroni. The palazzos are from the 14th and 15th centuries so you are sitting in an open air museum.

In the mornings there are usually a couple of market stalls, fruit and vegetables, fish and clothes.

Momento di Mindfulness
Laurels and Learning

Occasionally in Santa Margarita you may see students who have just graduated that day who are walking around celebrating with their families. The Italian graduates don't wear the mortar board hat of the English graduate but instead wear a real, authentic laurel leaf 'crown'. The laurel leaves are twisted together and are just like the ones you might see on a Roman statue.

Take this as a cue to spend a few seconds considering your own skills and achievements. Celebrate your own learning and think widely about practical skills as well as academic achievements. Give yourself some 'virtual laurels' and celebrate your skill. Sometimes it is hard to celebrate our own achievements. It's important to do this but it doesn't always come easily and needs to be worked on (as a skill!) If that is the case and focusing on your own learning is just too difficult then return to this another day. Instead today celebrate the success in learning of someone you know and award them the 'virtual laurel leaves'.

Campo Santo Stefano
For a campo on the main thoroughfare between San Marco and Accademia Campo Santo Stefano has a definite local character. It is a large and surprisingly quiet space.

Sometimes at Christmas it is home to a small market. In the summer there are usually some fringe Pavilions linked to the Biennale Art or Architecture. The Art Institute just off the corner of the square may be open for a free display of sculpture or a small entry fee display. It is worth spending time there because of the wonderful building and the views through its ancient Venetian glass windows.

If you walk into the campo from the Accademia Bridge you will pass the church of San Vidal. It is one of the Chorus Churches and was re-built in the seventeenth century. It has a different, light, airy and more modern feel than many of the churches. On an evening you may hear music drifting out from one of the concerts by Interpreti Veneziani with pieces by Bach, Vivaldi, Corelli and others. Like the church the music is light and familiar and so accessible for those who maybe only occasionally 'dip into' classical music.

Look out for the Art Institute with a small florists just outside its gates. The Gothic palazzo with it's beautiful glass windows always catches the attention. In a different way the florist gives us art to appreciate at a more basic human level and the seasonal selection of flowers is ever changing. This corner of Venice is a lovely place to gaze and attend to small details in a mindful way.

Apparently once there was bull fighting in the square. It's so hard to believe that now. It is a busy, yet not overcrowded, local centre. Donna Leon's Commissario Brunetti is called to a murder in this square in a novel which is set at Christmas. A street trader is murdered and a murky tale of blood diamonds, assassinations and mercenaries ensues. Rest assured Santo Stefano is a quiet and peaceful place even though it is very close to some of the busiest tourist destinations in the city.

As you walk through the campo you will notice a statue to the academic Niccolo Tommaseo who was one of those who was prominent in the Daniele Manin uprising when Venice rebelled against the Austrians. He was responsible for education in that brief resurrection of a new Venetian Republic. Manin was exiled from Venice after the Austrians took power again but is remembered for his essay writing and passionate commitment to an independent Venice.

Towards the northern end of the campo is the church of Santo Stefano. This was originally a monastery church and has cloisters as mentioned earlier in the section on walks centred around cloisters. There is a moving depiction of Jesus in the garden of Gethsemane by Tintoretto. The Church was built in the thirteenth century and has been added to over the centuries giving it a definite feeling of Gothic 'flair'. The difference between San Vidal at one end of the campo and San Stefano makes an interesting contrast.

Le Cafe
However, feeling a little guilty I have to admit that my favourite place in this campo is far more modern. It is the simply named 'Le Cafe' and describes itself as a bar, cafetria and sala de tea. We discovered it some years ago on a winter's night when we were waiting to go to a concert at San Vidal. It was busy, vibrant with light and airy cream interior, at that point featuring cherubs. Le Café always showcases the work of local artists. It offers tea, coffee, hot chocolate and even hot orzo for those who prefer a caffeine free alternative. And then there is the glass

of Prosecco or Spritz option. There is an array of hand made cakes - it's a true patisserie.

There are cafes and cafes. This one is special. Le Cafe is not cheap or inexpensive but neither is it Florians. In the winter you can sit inside and keep warm and have a true tea room experience. In the summer you can sit under a shady umbrella and watch the passers-by and life in the campo. Near my home town we have a world famous Cafe called Betty's Tea Room. If you ever visit York you will see the queue of people waiting to go into Bettys. My family call Le Cafe the Venetian Betty's. Interestingly Betty's was founded by an Austrian and there is an Austrian influence in Venice following the occupation. One of the more positive legacies may be the patisserie. Le Cafe is always on our Venice itinerary.

Momento di Mindfulness
Knitting and Newspapers

Jan Morris talks of 'knitting and newspapers' outside houses. It made me realise that Venice is still a place where you find newspaper and magazine stalls in most campos. These are usually rotunda shaped. Although Morris felt little had changed between her visits I don't recall seeing knitting on a chair outside a house in a campo in recent years. I do recall seeing three chairs in a row close to a bar with names painted on the back for the local retired men to use when they visited 'their local' bar. Life and living continues. Somehow the city needs to find a way for the profits of tourism to be ploughed into supporting and preserving the life of the locals, whether it is in housing/rents or making sure that local businesses like ironmongers (hardware stores), shoe shops, dry cleaners and undertakers keep in business. Venice is it's people. Their Veneziano, their community and unique approach to living.

Spend some time looking at one of the paper stalls. Maybe buy a local language paper or Italian magazine. It helps with language learning and also gives an insight into local concerns. It was from looking at notice boards in supermarkets that I learned about the concerns about cruise ships and the Giudecca Canal. I also learned that there is a need for dog walkers in Venice! It would also be possible to quickly find someone to give a language lesson.

We found out about the Advent concerts at San Trovarso from a poster on a door. I'd done the usual internet search looking for a more individual musical concert and found nothing. Venice is still a place where posters and notice boards are an important way of communicating about 'what's going on' that week.

Campo Santa Maria Formosa
This campo is where I usually sit down at the cafe in the shade and ask for a Lemon Soda. I've usually been walking a long way and my feet have started to ache. I persuade myself that Lemon Soda with its slightly bitter flavour is better for me than it probably is - after many visits to Italy a Lemon Soda is my firm favourite non-alcoholic beverage.

It's always a pleasure to sit and look at the ancient buildings and watch the Venetian world go by. It's a late afternoon/ early evening experience depending on the time of year and when dusk falls. A sunny afternoon in winter and a hot summer's day makes no difference. This campo is the true centre of a locality and the locals meet, greet and talk together while the children play football and the babies in strollers are admired by family and friends. Close by are the shops needed for daily living, like the local hardware and ironmongers, the bakery and the greengrocers.

This campo is never deserted, but is far enough away from the main tourist trails to be much quieter than other places. The Church has an interesting history. Legend has it that it was originally built in 639 by Magno di Oderzo who had a vision of a vague hazy outline of a voluptuous woman (formosa) who he realised was Mary. Like other churches the first documents are from around 1060 (around the time of the Norman Conquest in England).

The first church was destroyed by a fire in 1106 and then remodelled again in 1492 to give a more Renaissance architectural style. The campanile is lovely Baroque building dating back to 1688. It took a long while to build as it was designed by the priest Francesco Zucconi in 1611. I had always thought the elephant which escaped from a ship on the Riva degli Schiavoni in 1817 had ended up here, but I was wrong and that poor creature ended its brief escape in the Church of San Antonin, not far away in Castello. The remains of the elephant were taken to the university of Padua it's skeleton still remains.

Once a year the Doge went to pray in Santa Maria Formosa, to commemorate how Doge Pietro III Candiano rescued twelve girls who had been kidnapped by Istrian pirates. This event became the Feast of Mary which is still celebrated and has evolved to be called the Festa de le Marie de Tole, because wooden representations of the girls are carried as part of the celebration.

The Church does have an unusually impressive artwork depicting a woman. This is not a demure Madonna. George Sand mentions "an almost unique presentation of a hero woman". St Barbara is shown as a powerful force. The artist was Palma Il Vecchio and the inspiration may be his daughter Violante, who is said to have been 'beloved of Titian". On the altar is a sculpture of a fallen St Barbara with her head separate following decapitation by her father. Barbara's story certainly resembles Greek mythology. A daughter locked in a tower, miraculous transportation to the safety of a mountain gorge. Then betrayal by one of the shepherds who was turned to stone and whose flock were turned into locusts. Barbara was tortured and thrown into prison but didn't lose her faith and every night the cell was bathed in healing light and her wounds from torture disappeared. After being sentenced to death her father carried out the beheading himself and was then struck by lightning and consumed by flames as he journeyed home.

The very individual bookshop Aqua Alta is close to this campo. Here all the books are kept in watertight receptacles, including old Gondolas to keep them safe from high tides and flooding. If you wander through the shop you reach a room filled with piles of old books and a view out onto the canal. If you search on line you will find more specific information and directions about this book shop. I've certainly replenished my collection of Donna Leon's novels there. It's a mixture of new and second hand books and an English language guide books and some of the more individual guides like 'Secret Venice' by Thomas Jonglez can be found here.

There is a mystery about a carving on the entrance to the bell tower. It was described by Ruskin as grotesque and some think it is there to prevent the devil entering the tower to play the bells. Others see a resemblance to the Elephant Man who was deformed by neurofibromatosis or Von Recklinhausen's syndrome. The sadness is perhaps there was someone with this disability whose appearance was used to represent the devil. A moment for a sad and poignant reflection if that is the case.

Momento di Mindfulness
Cafe in Campo

Sit at a 'Cafe in a Campo'. Watch the world go by until someone comes to take your order. There is a cafe in Santa Maria Formosa which you can't miss. In the late afternoon you will share the cafe with the people who live in or near the square.

Order a drink. For me it would be cappuccino in the morning and then a large bottle of sparkling water or lemon soda or a prosecco/spritz in the late afternoon. It doesn't matter as long as it is a drink you can 'make last' while you 'watch the world go by.

While you drink utilise the approach of the 'raisin exercise' which is included in mindfulness courses. Each movement as you eat the raisin is considered with focus. Do the same with your drink.

Pick up the glass. Feel the temperature of the glass. Hold the glass. Lift it to your lips. Pause. Take a sip. Taste. Take another sip. Focus as the liquid moves over your palate to the back of your mouth and you automatically trigger a swallow. Pause again and repeat the movements.

If you have a straw and a can then imagine yourself moving in slow motion as you take the paper off the straw and click the can and put the straw into drink. Take a sip from the straw and sip again and notice when you swallow the fluid.

You are in a Venetian campo mindfully drinking coffee or soda and watching the world go by. This is something to add to your gratitude list. If you don't have a gratitude or happiness list then this is a good place to start one

Museo Querini Stampalia
This museum and gallery is found on small canal next to the Campo Santa Maria Formosa. Donna Leon's Brunetti calls in here one day and spends some moments lost in consideration of history through art. Brunetti feels this is a special place for Venetians, unlike the Accademia and other galleries and feels compelled to visit every so often. It is a special place. The house is set up as if it is frozen in a

moment in time, giving insight into how the family lived. The rooms on the upper floors are set up with items from the Querini family, furniture, china, chandeliers, sculptures as well as paintings. The art is impressive. Bellini's Presentation at the Temple is the most well-known but can often be on loan to other galleries. There are also works by artists like Giordano, Tiepolo and very Venetian scenes by Pietro Longhi.

The museum also has a collection by Gabriel Balla (born in 1730) filling a whole room. This series of paintings shows a year in the life of Venice with scenes covering all the major fairs and events which people of the time would have visited.

The ground floor is unique architecturally and was adapted in 1947 by Carlo Scarpa architects using water brought into the building to create a beautiful and accessible Japanese garden. This seems also to be with the intention of reducing the effects of Acqua Alta flooding. Water enters from the canal through water gates along the inner walls. In the garden is a many-levelled copper basin made from cement and mosaic and a little channel with two labyrinths sculpted in alabaster with sides of Istrian stone. The museum also has a café where the food and coffee get good reviews and of course a gift show to browse.

Momento di Mindfulness
Depth & Distance

Lorin Roche's more multi-sensory approach to meditation focuses on the lesser known sense of perceiving depth perception and distance. If you bounce a ball you have a sense which predicts the depth and strength of the 'bounce back' of the ball. How far objects are from us in space and how our perception of this might vary.

Think about a campo in terms of spaciousness and the contrast between warm, living spaces and true emptiness.

Focus on the objects in the space near you. This might be buildings, birds, people, tables, chairs or trees. Look at the colour and shape and the surfaces of the objects. Now focus on depth and distance. The distance of the objects from you. The depth or height between you and the objects. Consider the objects and their position in the space around you.

Close your eyes and open them again. Is anything different?

Campo San Giovanni e Paulo

The Venetians contract the name to San Zanipolo in Veneziana dialect. This campo is close to the Fondamenta Nuovo and the various vaporetto and ferry stations. In fact you may mistake the entrance to the hospital (Ospedale) for a church. It is the Renaissance Scuole Grande do San Marco. It must be the most impressive hospital entrance in the world. It's on a canal and not all the campos have that closeness to the canal which gives San Zanipolo a much more open feel to other campos.

There is an impressively tall bronze statue of a man and horse by Andrea Del Verrocchio. The figure is Bartolomeo Corleoni who died in 1475. The basilica of San Giovanni e Paulo is worth wandering into for its soaring ceilings. It took a hundred years to build and is the largest church in Venice completed in 1430. It's a Gothic church made of simple brick containing art work by Bellini and Veronese. It was the burial place for many rich and famous Venetians of the Republic. There are at least twenty five Doges and other leading Venetians interred here.

If you visit in the early spring then look out for the cafe and chocolatier Rosa Salva, 'cioccolato e pralinarier' is such a wonderful expression. It's a place to stop for a drink or to simply look at the lovely window display. At other times of the year you will have to make do with an award winning pastry.

 *Momento di Mindfulness*
Scents and Sites – 'Esscential' Sites

Follow a scent you notice (and like!) and just around the corner you may find:

Patticceria – warm pastries and cakes
Pizza or Foccacia with strongly smelling Oregano
Canals - salty sea of the lagoon

One of my favourite memories is noticing the smell of Christmas Panettone from an artisan bakers near to the Ca Fujiyama tea rooms. The smell of freshly baked Panettone permeated the whole street. It was the same in the days leading up to Easter. People buying their Panettone and wishing each other 'Buone Pasqua' or 'Buone Natale'.

Musical Soundscape

A Soundtrack for a city

Little is known of the early music of Venice. However in Renaissance and Baroque music it is incomparable. Here three Venetian composers are showcased as a musical soundtrack and a modern interpretation of Venetian music in a soundtrack.

Venice needs a soundtrack. It inevitably pulls on Baroque influences. That music still captures the beat and rhythm of the city. Once we stood in a small campo near the Frari Church and listened to a lute being played. It's eerie minor key melody taking us back in time.

Viva Vivaldi

Antonio Vivaldi, the red headed priest who only ever served a few masses before being released from duty due to chest constricting asthma. He became musical director at the Pieta. Here it becomes an inspirational story as the choir consisted entirely orphaned girls.

All four choral parts of works like the various Gloria were sung by women and that includes the Bass line. All the instruments in the accompanying orchestra were also played by women.

What an awesome 'girl power' sound they must have made. The church of the Pieta is on the Riva degli Schiavoni looking out into the Bacino and you can imagine sounds escaping out into the street and lagoon.

Vivaldi was born in 1678 and died in 1741. He composed, he was a multi-talented violinist, teacher and priest. He is Mr Baroque personified. Some say he churned out music and re-used sections but he was making a living as a composer and did what he needed to and others have done the same since.

For me Vivaldi's choral pieces move in musical history from the simple plainsong type of Gregorian Chant choral music to a more dynamic sound full of energy with the four different but connected sections of the choir moving in a counterpoint which blends together beautifully. We are not yet into the romance of chords which was to come later in musical history. Each line intersects and mirrors or leads and the effect is uplifting. In the famous Gloria in D Major the range of moods created for each part of the prayer are different. It works.

There is something about being on the lagoon or on a canal and imagining the driving opening bars of 'Gloria, Gloria in Excelsis Deo'. Listen and listen again.

The Gloria in D Major and the Four Seasons will give you a Venetian inspired meditational soundtrack.

The following Concertos are a good atmospheric introduction to Baroque music and extend your Venetian soundtrack.

- Lute and 2 Violins and Continuo in D Major RV 93 Allegro
- Lute in D Major, RV 93 Largo
- 2 Mandolins, Strings and Continuo in G, R.532 Andante

All are easily located on music streaming services or YouTube.

Gloria in D major works through several tempos and moods to reflect each line of the prayer/anthem. The vibrant start with 'Gloria in Excelsis Deo' is often used as background music for documentary films about the city. This has an orchestral introduction which is like a Venetian trumpet fanfare. It's difficult to hear the music without seeing floating scenes of the lagoon and islands. 'Et in Terra pax hominibus' was used to great effect in a short film about the devastating Aqua Alta of Autumn 2018 when San Marco was submerged to unprecedented levels. This music has a melancholy yet driving force propelling it.

'Domine Deus Rex Coelestis' is lovely to have in your mind while sitting on a wooden bench/ pew in a church looking up at painting ceilings and high rising rafters. At times the voice almost spirals up higher and higher towards the heavens while the oboe plays a lower more earthly tone. Contrasting with this beautiful melancholy piece is the choral fast moving 'Domine File Unigenite' with the different parts chasing each other in a driving powerful rhythm. All the parts fading and falling together towards the end.

'Qui tollis peccata mundi' is a short quieter prayerful almost pleading prayer for deliverance. In the final piece 'Cum Sancto Spiritu' all the moods of vibrancy in brass, the pulsing rhythm of the strings and the echoing voices in an Amen is almost a Redentore - hope and redemption. It's compelling as it works so well with the city landscape and history. Oh to hear it sung by a choir in the city! Perhaps one day...

The Four Seasons - Quattro Stagione
The Largo from Winter in the Four Seasons is one of my all-time favourite pieces of music. Before I knew it was Vivaldi I heard it and loved it. The concerto is based on four poems, possibly written by Vivaldi. They follow as part of a longer meditational activity. It's a short piece of music with varied pace and moods. Recently Max Richter and Nigel Kennedy have re-worked the Four Seasons and we all continue to be intrigued and inspired by the music.

Many years ago we visited Venice at New Year and on New Year's Eve went to a concert at San Vidal. It was a lovely evening, with hot chocolate at a cafe in Santa Stefano Campo, before going to the 'concerto'. This music is lovely and whether you listen to it live in a concert or stream it you can still become absorbed and imagine the different seasons. The icicles and ice breaking in winter, the ploughing the fields in the spring, the long hot days of summer and the fading warmth and changing colours of autumn. If landscape and music were to work in harmony then this is it at its best. Apparently it wasn't set in Venice but the wider Veneto region. I'm ignoring that - the minor melancholy Largo just has to be Venetian.

Vivaldi died away from Venice in an unmarked grave in Vienna - sad ending to a vibrant musical life.

Momento di Mindfulness
City Soundtrack

If you have access to the technology on your mobile phone then download Vivaldi's Gloria in D. Why not listen to it on headphones while you ride up the Grand Canal or along the Bacino past San Marco. A mindful interlude watching Venice with a Venetian Soundscape. If you don't have the technology and headphones then listen before you go out and imagine the harmonies while walking around the city.

Albinoni and his Adagios
Sometimes for me I have a day where 'it has to be' Albinoni's music. Those dark moods and minor keys of his compelling Adagios help me work through difficult days. The music reminds me of much later works by Rachmaninov and Morricone's score to the movie 'The Mission'. I suspect Albinoni's influence is greater than we realise. If you search you should find an inexpensive collection called Albinoni's Adagios on CD or streaming with a picture of Venice on the cover.

Bach was certainly influenced by Albinoni. He composed fugues based on his work. These being a Fugue in A major on a theme by Tomaso Albinoni, BWV 950, and Fugue in B minor on a theme by Tomaso Albinoni, BWV 951.

Tomaso Albinoni was born in Venice in June 1671. His Adagio in G Minor may or may not have been written by him; but current evidence is veering towards it being authentic. Much of his work was lost over time and in the second world war bombing of Dresden. Like Vivaldi he died in obscurity though this time it was in Venice in the parish of San Barnaba.

Majestic Monteverdi
Claudio Monteverdi was born in 1567 and bridged the transition between Renaissance and Baroque music. He moved to Venice to be Master of Music at San Marco and stayed there until he died. His music is haunting in its style of choral music with a solo tenor voice rising above the other voices. It feels like the majestic music of a Tudor court. Monteverdi is buried in the Frari Church. His choral music is for me the most beautiful with music at Vespers. One year when we were in the Salute at Christmas we noticed the service of Verspers with an organ recital. Echoes of Monteverdi can still be found in Venice.

Soundtrack to Casanova

The only time we visited Venice at the end of August was the year that the movie Casanova was showcased at the Venice Film Festival. It was an amazing evening. Hot and arid during the day and then cloud burst of a thunder storm at dusk. Heath Ledger and Sienna Miller were probably there. The reception for the film was in the Doge's palace.

There were flaming torches along the portico outside the Doge's palace making it incredibly atmospheric. If you are looking for an individual soundtrack then it is worth considering this film score. Alexandre Desplat's score features classical composers such as Vivaldi, Albinoni and Rameau with some minor re-arrangements. There are also some original compositions by Desplat which merge well with the original music of the time. This Casanova falls in love with the feminist writer played by Sienna Miller – so a modern twist to a tale of its time.

 Momento di Mindfulness
Raising the Roof

Rooftops and skyline

Imagine Casanova escaping from prison, up and out of the dungeons and out over the rooftops. Imagine that soundtrack of Baroque music accompanying this hair raising exploit. A much more spacious view than the prison cell.

Part 11

EARLY EVENING /DUSK

"In the glare of the day there is little poetry about Venice, but under the charitable moon her stained palaces are white again..."

Mark Twain

Is yours a Prosecco, Spritz or Bellini ?

As late afternoon passes into early evening it's the time for an 'apparetivo'. Hopefully its warm enough to sit outside and feel just a little Venetian.

Analcolica Alternatives

Any bar should have a range of fruit juice and the special combination drinks, served to resemble a cocktail which the Italians call 'analcolica'. The English equivalent is Mocktails which are increasing in popularity.

Prosecco

Prosecco is served at bars by the glass. At a bar like Nico's on the Zattere you see and hear the constant popping of new bottles. The large glasses let you 'swirl and sip' as the bubbles hit the back of your palate. There are many lovely 'aparativos' but I prefer just 'plain Prosecco' and guess I always will. I've yet to track down the Venetian 'cloudy Prosecco' mentioned in cookery books and on recipe sites. The Veneto is the home of Prosecco - it is very much a Venetian drink.

The Spritz'
Aperol Spritz

If you look closely at what people are drinking as they sit talking at bars in the late afternoon and evening then you will see this vibrant orange coloured drink. It has an unusual sweet almost aniseed like aroma. Aperol is something you can almost persuade yourself is healthy as it is an infusion of herbs and is a light liqueur at around 11% alcohol The two distinctive flavours are orange and rhubarb. The bright orange Aperol is mixed with sparkling prosecco and soda or mineral water. It can be made with the still white wine of the Veneto if you don't want the fizz. It's usually garnished with a slice of lemon. On a hot day the contrasting bitterness and sweetness is refreshing.

Campari Spritz

Like Aperol Campari is made from an infusion of herbs and fruit. I have no idea what Chinotto and Cascarilla are but they are in it. There is a Chinotto flavoured San Pellegrino soft drink which is bitter in flavour. Campari is dark red and mixed with the prosecco and soda or mineral water and is bitter with a little less sweetness than an Aperol spritz.

Bellini
Bellini is served in a flute glass. This is a simple combining of peach purée and prosecco. It was named Bellini as the pink colour resembled a toga in a painting by the artist Bellini. It became a popular seasonal drink at the famous Harry's Bar. It is traditionally made with white peaches. Soda or mineral water can be used to make a non-alcoholic version.

Negroni
Beware, this vintage cocktail is much more alcoholic. Negroni is made with equal parts gin, vermouth and Campari. The vermouth varies and many use sweet Cinzano Rosso. Some bars serve a 'sbagliato' or 'mistaken' Negroni, with prosecco added instead of gin.

Zattere Sunset
Walking along the Zattere is special at any time of day. In the morning the bright sunlight spreads and reflects in every direction. However as a clear day draws to a close a beautiful sunset can light up the horizon toward the mainland. Settling into a bar or restaurant along the Zattere is a perfect way to relax and watch the sunset.

219

 *Momento di Mindfulness*
Sundown breeze

It's a curious thing that if you are on the Zattere at sunset you may well experience a breeze which lasts just a short time as the last rays of the sun set for the day. I've never read anything about it, but I've experienced it enough times to know it happens.

At the end of the day as the sun begins to set start to notice the first lights and lanterns coming on. Another transition time.
Watch the sunset, notice the breeze and look for the first lights to be switched on ready for dusk. That's a multi-sensory mindful moment.

Of course I'd also suggest this is a cue to put some insect repellent on your arms and ankles if you are visiting in hot weather. The lovely transition between sunset and dusk is the time when the mosquitos start to appear and it's wise to have protective repellent.

Cucina Veneziana - Take a Taste

Radicchio do Treviso
Radicchio is a vegetable we never get in Northern England where I live. There is a bitter red lettuce which uses the name, but I now know this really is nothing like the Venetian Radicchio. In December this vegetable was piled high in the Supermercato in Venice. It was the vegetable provided with most of our meals out - including our Christmas Dinner at Antica Locanda Montin. It was bitter but delicious. Pliny the Elder in his *Naturalis Historia* mentioned the "Venetian lettuce" emphasizing its purifying health qualities.

Radicchio is grown in the province of Venice in the Veneto especially around Treviso and is more properly called Radicchio di Treviso. There is a more expensive white version which was first produced in the nineteenth century. However I now recognise the type we ate last December; it was the late red radicchio (radicchio rosso tardivo di Treviso). It has long and slender fronds with white centres and red, dark crimson edges to the leaves. It is a true winter taste from November to the spring. It is prized in a risotto.

Vino - Ombre
Any time, any place, take an ombre which is a small glass of wine.

Venetian Dishes
Venetian cooking has its roots in seafood, Middle Eastern dishes and preserved food. The Venetians became leaders in salt production so were able to preserve food more successfully than other city states.

There is also an emphasis on food grown in the surrounding area. Vegetables such as peas, beans, asparaguses, artichokes and radicchio appear in Venetian recipes.

Rice is more common here due to the paddy fields in the Po estuary. Or is that due to Marco Polo's travels? As in all Northern Italy, though, Polenta is a staple food. In Venice the Polenta grains are ground into much smaller fragments so it has the texture of a pudding.

A Selection of La Serenissima's Signature Dishes:

Cicchetti & Crostini
The fame of these small sized snacks has grown rapidly in recent years. They are often found in the traditional small 'Bacaro'. We've already mentioned these in an earlier section of *'Exploring Venice'*

Crostini might have toppings of creamed cheese, cured meat, pesto, olive or redcurrant. Cicchetti might have salt cod or blue cheese or cannellini beans with garlic. The range is varied between bars and is endless.

Saor in Sarde
This has its roots in preserved food of Medieval times. Sailors and fisherman would take this dish out to sea with them. Fried sardines are marinated in balsamic vinegar, onions, raisins and pine nuts. There is a curious mix of sour and sweet flavours in this dish. It seems fishermen used vinegar to preserve fish which is how the dish developed over time.

Baccala mantecato
This is another dish with its roots in food preservation. This is creamed, dried cod prepared by soaking, broiling and blending the fish into a smooth mousse. This is then seasoned with olive oil, salt and pepper. Sometimes herbs like parsley and garlic are added. It's served spread on fresh bread or polenta.

Risotto Nero
Risotto is Venetian. As a child I stayed in a hotel in Lido di Jesolo where the impact of the concept of giving English visitors the same as they ate at home had not yet reached. Thank Goodness. For evening meal in the Hotel Vianello we had a risotto made with kidneys and parmesan and I still remember it nearly fifty years later. I recently tried to re-create my memory of the dish at home. I'm still working on it!

Seafood risotto is Venetian. Risotto can often be jet-black. The risotto is salty with squid, wine, onion, tomato and the black squid ink.

Risi e Bisi
Risi e bisi is simple dish of rice and peas. On April 25, St. Mark's Day, this dish was presented to the Doge by people from the lagoon islands.

Risi e bisi is made with rice, pancetta, onion, butter, parsley and a stock made with pea shells. It's runnier than a risotto and thicker than a soup. It's seasonal and served at the time of the pea harvest

Calf liver and stewed onions.
Liver is combined with sweet, caramelized onion and served on a bed of polenta.

Moleche are small green crabs with no shell. They are another seasonal dish. The window for Moleche is narrow as the crab shell hardens eventually.

Baicoli. Among the most important rations for Venetian ships were the dry, oval-shaped, long lasting baicoli (a kind of ship's biscuits). The biscuits look simple but preparing them is actually a long process because baicoli need two rises and double baking. Many a Venetian noble was fond of dipping baicoli in cream or dessert wines. These days you'll generally find them served with coffee and zabaglione.

Minestra de Pasta e Fasioi. Pasta and Bean Soup is a very thick bean soup with pasta.

Polenta a Schie
Schie are a tiny shrimp which is only found in the Venetian lagoon. Schie are seasoned with lemon, garlic, pepper and salt, then fried and served with polenta.

Browsing Books at La Toletta

In my favourite corner of Dorsoduro is a rather special bookshop. Browsing the shelves of La Toletta is always worthwhile. La Toletta is a bookshop which was founded in 1933 by Angelo Pelizzato and is the oldest bookshop in the city. It is also now a publishing house having published more than 150 books with a focus on Venice.

La Toletta is increasingly a cultural centre with its Spazio Eventi. Events might include book presentations or debates. There is the possibility of a literary café. In the days when bookshops are struggling across Western Europe the move to widen scope, but still keep books at the centre of La Toletta's philosophy makes a lot of sense.

I was intrigued to learn that after 8th September 1943 when Italy left the war and became an occupied country that Angelo used La Toletta as a communication hub for the partisans. It seems from the website that there were 'weapons for the partisans and clandestine magazines.' hidden among the books on the shelves.

Browse La Toletta today and you will probably find a treasure of an unusual book about the city or an English language novel to read while you are on vacation. I am something of a stationery collector and the range of pens, mugs and bags with a literary theme makes this a good place to shop for souvenirs.

On reflecting on the books about Venice I've read and enjoyed I would showcase three authors. Sally Vickers caught the spirit of the city in her novel '*Miss Garnet's Angel*'.

Sarah Dunnant is a favourite writer of historical fiction as the writing is always of a literary quality. In a Guardian Review in 2006 the reviewer writes of the novel '*In the Company of the Courtesan*' that "16th century Venice comes to life convincingly. Her skill is evident in the fact that the 'real' characters - including the writer and 'scourge of princes' Pietro Aretino, and the painter Titian - do not seem out of place among their fictional counterparts."

Donna Leon has written a series of over 25 novels about the fictional Guido Brunetti and his life as a Commissario of police. I've found that over the years her writing has strengthened my knowledge and understanding of Venice. The offshoot 'Brunetti's Walks' by Tony

Sepeda is a guide book with a difference and was a wonderful way of structuring one of our holidays in Venice. I am aware that I've referred to Donna Leon several times in '*Exploring Venice*'. I've reflected on this and decided that because the novels have given such an insight into the city, its culture and cuisine (as well as pleasure in reading the novels) that inclusion is as appropriate as that of Ruskin or Morris.

La Toletta is publishing some fiction now and long may this continue. There are never enough stories set in La Serenissima.

Sgroppino & Sorbet Somewhere
In the summer a sorbet is my 'go to' dessert choice. Somehow even the pre-made sorbets in the supermarkets in France and Italy taste authentic. A scoop or two of lemon sorbet sitting outside in the shade at a cafe on a hot August afternoon is a wondrously reviving. Of course sorbet has that 'palate clearing quality' at any time of the year. Yoghurt ice cream is growing in popularity in Italy but my preference is for the clear and sharp tasting sorbet.

Sgroppino is a frothy mixture of lemon sorbet and prosecco. Sgropino is Venetian and originates in the 16th century for refreshing the palate between the fish and meat course.

In Venetian dialect Sgroppino means "to untie" and it does release and relieve the full feeling of over indulgence.

Sometimes nowadays a small amount vodka is added or the prosecco substituted by champagne. It needs to be Venetian and authentic and simply refreshing.

Carnevale
The Carnival of Venice (*Carnevale di Venezia*) is an annual festival. Carnivale leads up to Lent. Festivals like Mardi

Gras on Shrove Tuesday (*Martedì Grasso*). Before the rigours and restrictions of Lent in my own country the butter and cream is used up in pancakes. In Venice richness of the feasting, dancing and masked identities became frantic in seeking pleasure before Lent began.

The roots of Carnivale may be in 1162 when celebration of a victory against Aquileia happened at this time of year with dancing and celebration in San Marco. At various points the Carnivale has been utilised as 'a way of saving the city's prosperity'. In the seventeenth century during the height of Venetian Baroque the Carnivale was reinforced as a way of attracting visitors. Once Venice was occupied by Austria then Carnivale was banned. Even masks were forbidden. There is some evidence of some Carnival activities in the nineteenth century but nothing like an organised annual festival.

In the years following the great flood of 1966 and the beginning of the Venice in Peril Fund a new type of Carnivale began to return as a focus of fund raising. Masks began to appear again. As well as mass produced masks the skilled craft of mask making was resurrected. By1979 the Carnivale was again a structured event. Nowadays, Carnevale goes on for two weeks with masked balls, candlelight procession of boats, concerts, street art and performances.

Momento di Mindfulness
Masks and Masking

Find a mask somewhere which appeals to you in design, colour and shape.

There are easily available workshops where you can actually make your own mask. There are bespoke craft designs and mass produced masks. There are miniature masks as badges and fridge magnets. There are masks to wear to masked balls. It really doesn't matter what you choose.

You may find an image of a mask in an online search. There are many ways to locate a design which you like. You have another souvenir to take home with you.

Think of the traditional masks of the contrasting 'Happy and Sad' faces (traditionally these are for drama comedy and tragedy). Note down quickly what is currently making you happy in your life and what is making you feel somewhat sad. Hopefully there is little making you sad while on your vacation.

Emotional Resilience and Intelligence is sometimes about keeping calm and focused even when you are in a difficult conversation at work or at home. Make a mental picture of your 'mask'. Carry this mental picture with you so when you need a boost to your resilience you can remember it and visualise it to give you confidence when you need to be positive and assertive. The distraction of the mask may well reduce any anxiety levels when you are in situations where you need an extra boost of resilience in the months ahead. When you need to combine the image of your mask with conscious slow and steady breathing.

Bright Beads

Venetian beads and jewellery give a link back to the opulence of the later years of the Republic. Many are made with glass which contains minerals making the glass glisten in light. There is often gold and the settings of jewellery in the shops on the Rialto are not usually demure. There is usually a certain Venetian flamboyance.

The glass necklaces and ear rings in shops or artisan websites give you an idea of the rich blues, greens and reds in the glass of the jewellery. Doing an online search for images of Venetian jewellery shows how uniqueness and vibrancy.

 Momento di Mindfulness
Imaginary Beads

Create an imaginary bowl of beads in your imagination as a focus for your attention. A mixture of coloured glass, with sparkling minerals embedded in the glass. Bright beads mixed together in a kaleidoscope of colour.

Imagine the colours mixing, merging and changing. Imagine them pastel coloured, vibrant and garish and greyscale in colour.

Look Up

It's dusk. The sun is setting. Sometimes as the shadows are taking over the landscape it can change the way we see things.

Look up at the skyline and the rooftops. Look at the roofs, the chimney pots. In Venice no roof or chimney pot ever seems the same.

A medieval, renaissance mismatch of styles which somehow fits together. Add in a 20th Century TV Aerial.

Close your eyes and open again. Can you almost imagine a man climbing over the roofs and escaping to freedom. Climbing, clambering over the terracotta tiles, laughing in the face of the fear of falling. Perhaps a cloak billowing around him. You are visualising the escape of Casanova from the dungeon, beginning his journey of exile to Paris. Was Casanova a secret agent of the Venetian Republic who was allowed by the authorities to escape – who knows. This legend of him escaping to freedom across the Venetian skyscape gives a moment to pause and imagine the scene.

Look up and keep looking up.

Part 12

DARKNESS & MIDNIGHT MUSINGS

"At the bridge I stood
lately in the brown night.
From afar came a song:
as a golden drop it welled
over the quivering surface.
Gondolas, lights, and music —
drunken it swam out into the twilight.
My soul, a stringed instrument,
sang to itself, invisibly touched,
a secret gondola song,
quivering with iridescent happiness.
— Did anyone listen to it?"

Friedrich Nietzsche

Dusk to darkness is one of those transformation points in the day which we are often too busy to notice. Sometimes it's twilight before we've realised the sun has set for the night. While on vacation focusing on sunrise and sunset adds depth and markers to your day. Even if you are only in a place for a day or two you will notice when it starts to grow lighter and the first rays of the sun brighten the room. Usually when I travel to Venice I have to change my watch by an hour so immediately time and perceptions change. Some will have a far greater time-change and the positive is that it does change perceptions and give a clear transition to 'vacation time'.

The intention in writing '*Exploring Venice*' was to share suggestions about special places to visit and add a layer of mindfulness to the experience. In this section it's the end of the day. The Venetian day followed from Dawn to Darkness is coming to an end. It will soon be time to sleep. This last section is about taking that one last evening walk, or just looking out of the window at the rooftops in the moonlight.

232

Momento di Mindfulness
Silhouette into Sunset

I remember one special day as the final rays of sunlight had faded when we could see both the sun and moon together in the sky. As the vaporetto chugged back to San Marco via San Giorgio one of the passengers pointed up to the sky. The passenger had never seen anything like this before and was very excited. Others started to look and take photos. I don't feel it's that unusual in the northern hemisphere where I live but it is certainly caused excitement and comment. Since that time I've noticed it happening a couple of times and it always reminds me of that vaporetto ride in Venice.

Softly Lit City
The sunlit city becomes a softly lit city. The lamplight is usually a gently subdued shade and lights are reflected on the dark waters of the canals. The calles, campiellos and sortoportogos look very different in lanternlight.

Local Language to inspire a Venetian Mantra
These words combine with alliteration and have a rhythmic, poetical quality. They may just be local words for walkways or types of canal but they sound inspiring in a mantra.

Calle, Campiello, Campo
Rio Tera, Rivo Ruga, Rughetto

Serene Salizzada, Silent Sortoportego
Ruga Rughetta, Rio Riva

There are lots of potential combinations for a mini break mantra.

Calle: street or alleyway
Campiello: small square
Campo: square
Corte: small square with buidings
Lista: near a foreign ambassador palace
Merceria: street lined with shops
Rio: small canal
Rio Terà: when a canal once was and is now filled with earth
Riva: street quay onthe lagoon or Canal Grande
Ruga: the first streets with houses and shops on both sides

Rughetta: small "ruga"
Salizzada: the first (important) streets to be paved
Sotoportego: passageway under a building

Shades and Shadows

It's strange but I have never felt safer in any city I've visited than in Venezia after dark. The city closes down fairly early in the evening in the winter months. There are hotspots of nightlife near the university and Campo Santa Margherita but overall the city is quiet safe and well-lit at night.

However as with many medieval cities the legends and ghost stories permeate through. Haunted Palazzos inflicting cursed luck to those who move in (Palazzo Dario). There is the legacy of anguish of the plague victims and the melancholy islands where they were taken for burial in mass graves. Bones are still never far from the surface on some of these islands.

The most famous grisly and gruesome tale is a 'Sweeny Todd' type tale about a butcher called Basio who lived in Santa Croce in the fifteenth century. Basio made sausages and meats which were often served with a highly flavoured sauce. Then someone found part of a finger with a nail attached which led to a police raid and discovery that Basio had been killing children and then adding body parts to his meat products. It is said he could not remember how many he had murdered.

234

Basio was beheaded in San Marco Piazza. I've never been to this vaporetto stop, but there is apparently a Riva de Basio boat stop. His house and shop are no longer there.

There are tales of suicide due to the unrequited love of a painter in the Casino degli Spiriti which means the small house of the spirits or souls. Also abusive jealous husbands who were so suspicious of their wives that they murdered them. Loredan, who beheaded his wife and then threw himself into the lagoon is the most famous. Loredan was sent to Rome to ask for redemption which was refused so he returned to Venice and committed suicide.

The tale of Othello full of doomed, obsessive love leading to the murder of Desdemona. This sad story about how manipulation can build images and stories which have no roots in reality and defeat trust and forgiveness in a relationship is Venetian. Desdemona's Palazzo is reportedly on the Grand Canal in the San Marco, opposite the Salute area.

If you want to know more about the shades and spirits haunting Venice then book onto a walking tour. These are easily found at Tourist information or via the internet. Of course the tours tend to take place by moonlight.

You will inevitably go to the Calle dei Assassini and discover how it became notorious for murders and muggings.

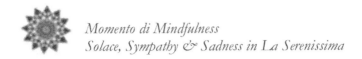

Momento di Mindfulness
Solace, Sympathy & Sadness in La Serenissima

Take a moment for compassionate thinking about those who died before their time in a violent and painful way. The grief and the anguish of those they leave behind. Give thoughts or prayers for solace for those living with sadness.

Feel 'thankfulness' for your day and the time spent exploring Venezia.

Venice By Moonlight - Moonlight cruise in Bacino or Canal
See the city lit up in a magical, reflective dark blue light. At any time of year the lights in the evening give the buildings that luminous, mirror like appearance.

- Take a vaporetto from Salute or Zattere to San Zaccaria.
- Take a vaporetto from Fondameta Nuove past Giardino to San Marco.
- If you can't go by boat and see the lights and the reflections in the lagoon then walk as far as you can on the Riva degli Schiavoni.
- Go to Rialto after 21:00 hrs and feel that you have the bridge to yourself.
- Take a vaporetto from Rialto to Accademia or further to Salute.
- Take a Vaporetto past the Casino stop up the Cannaregio Canal.

Walk, walk and walk some more. Make every moonlight moment count.

Momento di Mindfulness
Walk on the Riva degli Schiavoni

The lights which appear on an evening change the character of San Marco, the Riva and the Rialto Bridge. Sightseeing after dark is essential if you are staying in the city.

Sometimes, quite early in the evening we've had the Rialto Bridge almost to ourselves. It's more likely out of season but it will definitely be a more tranquil experience in the evening.

If you need to prioritise one of these then either walk from San Marco along the Riva to the Arsenale or vice-versa.

San Marco by Moonlight
Look at the lights in San Marco. A perfect symmetry of lamps amid the diffused light from the café-bars. Listen to the music from the small orchestras. Sway in time to the beat of the songs they play, usually easy listening from the 20th century.

Gaze at the Basilica and look up at the golden mosaics with the domes rising up into the (hopefully) moonlit sky.

Lamplit Lagoon
Walk from the Piazza out towards the Bacino. In the darkness this will often be silvery, reflected water. Still, luminous, dark waters with shadows of empty gondolas adding a dimension to the scene. Morris describes the 'Kaleidoscopic basin outside St Marks' and it is much more of a kaleidoscopic merging of colours and shapes in the evening.

All you need to do is walk and look at lights, the patterns they make on the buildings and canals. Consider how the lamps enlighten the city and somehow it seems a different city in greyscale without the ochres, teracottas, the warm white colours of the buildings and the everchanging greens and blues of the canals in daylight. Consider the contrast.

Feel the breeze. Focus on the way your feet move on the pavement. Breathe in and notice if you are breathing cold or warm air.

Candles and Candelabras

There is something very Venetian about candlelight and especially Candelabras giving soft golden light. Candelabras, brocade curtains and bedspreads in colours like golden ochre or red oxide colours. Venice is not a place for pastel furnishings. It is a city with its own colour scheme and I'm always disappointed if I stay in a room with modern furnishings.

If you are walking or travelling by vaporetto along the Grand Canal then look up at the Noble Floors of the Palazzos and notice the chandeliers. You may never see as many chandeliers again as you do in Venice.

At Christmas I substitute Christmas lights for chandeliers but it's the same exercise. Simply looking up and noticing the small details in the environment. Christmas lights shining out from the buildings along the Canale Grande.

Candlelight meditations can be a little tricky when travelling. I often take a travel candle or nightlight with me but I don't always use it, mostly as I worry that I may set off the fire alarm.

It's unlikely if the window is open and the room is well ventilated but I'm cautious nevertheless. Candle meditations are easily found online and that's probably the best option if you are staying in a hotel. If you are in an apartment then you can end the day with a candle flame meditation.

You will always find candles in bars and restaurants even if you are unable to end the day with a candle flame meditation. Take the opportunity for a short moment of meditation focusing on the flickering candle flame. Nothing simpler and a good way to end a day of sight seeing in La Serenissima.

Incense & Ancient Spices

Sometimes in a church you might catch a fleeting scent of incense. Perhaps it's from a recent service or maybe from centuries of priests diffusing incense in services so that it has soaked into the fabric and fittings of the church. Incense comes from the Latin 'to burn'.

If you look carefully close to an altar you might see a 'thurible' which is a decorative metal container with chains to hang it up which is used to burn incense.

In Venice the merchants returned with precious oils and spices from the Far East and Orient and these probably found their way into places of worship more easily than in other cities. Frankincense is the usual scent associated with churches.

Other oils are used in different religions. Oils and resins of cypress, cedar, sandalwood, clove, juniper, benzoin, myrrh, patchouli and sage all give off a woody and fragrant aroma.

I would choose Clary Sage or Germanium oil for diffusing. Rose Otto or Rose Damascena and Lavender blend very well with both Clary Sage and Geranium oils. Make your own individual and modern version of a spicy eastern scent. These oils are all beneficial for creating a calm serene mindset.

If you have one of the mini travel diffusers then you are ready to end each day with a fragrant oil. These seem to be widely available and reducing in price now they can be charged using USB cables.

Essential oils can be diffused or mixed with lotion or oil and used as a foot or body massage. Sometimes I just add to water and a few drops of essential oil to a spray bottle for a room spray or simple refreshing perfume.

 *Momento di Mindfulness*
Mindful Movie Memories

Take a moment to inhale the scent of an essential oil. If you are in a hotel then fill the sink or bidet with hot water and sprinkle 3 or 4 drops of each oil to vaporise and scent the room.

'And breathe' ... inhale the scent.

Create a calm, considered approach to living.

Make this a transition point at the end of the day before rest and sleep with anticipation of a new day tomorrow.

Movie Magic
Sit and play the movie of your the day in Venice in your mind. Visual images, thoughts, auditory soundtrack and symbols all merging together. Add an emotional overlay remembering how you felt at various points of the day. What emotion are you ending today with?

Mindfulness in action bringing 'special effects' to the scripts of our lives. **Making Mindful Movie Memories.**

Marangona at Midnight

One of the strongest peels of bells is at 6 o clock in the evening when every bell in the city seems to ring out. Except for the Campanile in San Marco that is. The only surviving original bell is called the Marangona. The Marangona is rung only at noon and midnight.

Bells were rung for centuries to mark the structured work day at Arsenale. Hundreds of workers moving through the streets towards the shipyard. Maybe scenes resembling a science fiction movie like 'metropolis'. Shared purpose and cohesion in building galleys for the Republic.

Open the window at midnight and see if you can hear the Marangona ringing out the new day.

If you go to San Marco at midnight in the summer you may still hear café orchestras playing, whereas in the winter you may see the Christmas or Carnivale lights sparkling across the piazza.

Spend a moment looking at the Basilica in darkness. The glittering domes of what is known locally as the 'Basilica of Gold'. Focus on glimmers and glittering in the darkness. A glimmer of hope is always welcome. Be hopeful for tomorrow. Listen out for the Marangona at Midnight.

Dark Hour

Deep dark
Dusk growing
Gathering up light
Deepening
Falling darkness
Enveloping, mysterious
Lights on darkness
Light reflecting
Lamps lightening
Lagoon landscape

Part 13

SCENIC SEASONAL SERENITY

*'sea-light and the evanescent mists ,
a meeting of land and sea,
East and West,'*

Salley Vickers

Seasons-Scape

This section has a different focus because it is about taking a seasonal perspective. A Venetian walk for each season is suggested along with a short seasonal description of the city. The words and music of Vivaldi's Four Seasons is used as the framework for this section. It's thought that Vivaldi wrote the words of the poem himself, though no one really knows.

The Four Seasons is a 'sound poem' and this section makes it the focus for a creative mindful meditational experience.

Spring

Venice in spring is about bright skies and a radiant blueness with fast moving clouds. Spring breezes but with some suddenly warm days. Of walks in San Polo and Castello with sight of wisteria and magnolia behind faded brick and stone walls.

Winter is shaking off its winter coat. There are fewer crowds and spring flowers. There may be rain but if you are lucky it will be a shower and the sun will soon shine through and dry off the wet paving stones.

April 25th is the Festa Di San Marco. It's the day when men traditionally give roses to the women in their lives. There is also a gondolier regatta between Sant'Elena island and Punta della Dogana. This is a bright day in that it is also Liberation Day celebrating the end of Nazi occupation in the Second World War.

Between May 31 to June 1 is the Marriage to the Sea ceremony when a laurel wreath is thrown into the lagoon at the Lido to symbolise the city's wedding to the sea. Holy Water indeed. A regatta follows.

The Vongalonga rowing event signals the end of Spring in early June. It's a 20-mile boat race between the islands and the Grand Canal and thousands of boats take to the water.

Sometimes you can see the Dolomite mountains in the distance. I remember this being pointed out to me by an elderly Italian lady when I was a small child. Generations of children have been shown 'the Dolomites' and the folklore about how these link with the weather and atmospherics. I think it means there may be rain – I'm not too sure!

Certainly from roof terraces there will be times when the Dolomites are visible and it is an unexpected and special sight. I first saw the mountains on the horizon in late Spring. It happens most during the bright, cold, windy days, often in winter and spring. There is a website in the Reference section which shows incredible photos of the Dolomites from Venice if you don't have a day when you can see the mountains.

Mindful Walking in Spring
If you are in Venice in the Spring then take a mindful walk. Whether it is in rain or sun take a walk on a spring day.

You can start either from San Marco and walk to the Rialto and make that your first tranche of the walk or start at Rialto. Cross the Rialto Bridge and then follow the signs for The Accademia.

Walk through San Polo and gaze at the medieval houses, campos and canals. See if you can spot the Fire station to your left as you move from San Polo into Dorsoduro. Perhaps stop at Tonolos or Bar Toletta for a coffee and a pastry.

Pause for a moment at the Grand Canal at Accademia. If you are tiring then take a boat from Accademia back to a stop close to where you are staying.

If you still have energy then cross the Accademia Bridge. As you move into Campo San Stefano you have a choice to make. You can walk past San Stefano Church and straight on (sempre dritto) back to the Rialto Bridge.

Or you can leave the campo at Le Café and follow the signs straight back to San Marco. It's a long walk but a lovely experience on a spring morning – especially between 7.30 and 9.00 a.m. before breakfast.

Spring – Concerto in E Major

Allegro
Springtime is upon us.
The birds celebrate her return with festive song,
and murmuring streams are softly caressed by the breezes.
Thunderstorms, those heralds of Spring, roar,

245

casting their dark mantle over heaven,
Then they die away to silence,
and the birds take up their charming songs once more.

Largo
On the flower-strewn meadow,
with leafy branches rustling overhead,
the goat-herd sleeps,
his faithful dog beside him.

Allegro
Led by the festive sound of rustic bagpipes,
nymphs and shepherds lightly dance
beneath the brilliant canopy of spring.

Summer

Listen to the music and drift and imagine summer days. In Venice that can be dry dusty days of seeking shade and staying out of the direct sun. The heat can be intense and the city almost deserted of locals during the hot Ferragosta days in August. Then a sudden dramatic thunder storm and sheet or jagged lightning washing the streets free of dust.

There can be some advantages to the summer. We've found bars like Nico's on the Zattere are quieter than in June or July. There is little shade but I rather like visiting Torcello on a hot day.

It's time to explore the city in the early morning before the heat rises. Or take an ice cream and a prosecco in the moonlight. Breakfast outside in a campo or a garden. Sitting outside on the back of a vaporetto with a breeze across the lagoon as you travel to the Lido. Again we've done this before breakfast in August.

Summer – Concerto in g-minor

Allegro non molto
Beneath the blazing sun's relentless heat
men and flocks are sweltering,
pines are scorched.
We hear the cuckoo's voice;

then sweet songs of the turtle dove and finch are heard.
Soft breezes stir the air….
but threatening north wind sweeps them suddenly aside.

The shepherd trembles,
fearful of violent storm and what may lie ahead.

Adagio e piano - Presto e forte
His limbs are now awakened from their repose
by fear of lightning's flash and thunder's roar,

as gnats and flies buzz furiously around.

Presto
Alas, his worst fears were justified,
as the heavens roar and great hailstones beat down
upon the proudly standing corn.

Mindful Walking in Summer:
If you are in Venice in the summer then take a walk (and a boat ride) before the heat of the day slows you down.

Start somewhere on the Zattere. San Basilio would give you the longest walk along the Zattere but you can start at any point on the Zattere.

Walk towards the Dogana right at the end of the Zattere. Hopefully the sun will be warming the Fondamenta and twinkling on the Giudecca Canal as you walk along the Zattere.

Pause at the Dogana and take in the views. Continue round to the Salute. Pause again for more views. Follow the signs for the Accademia.

247

If you are tiring then you can take a boat here to somewhere near where you are staying. If you have energy turn again towards the Zattere – it's very close and a straight walk through a number of streets. My favourite is to follow the signs from Accademia to the first canal and then turn left.

You will pass the Squero boat yard and San Trovarso with lovely canal views before you reach the Zattere again.

Make sure you take a coffee somewhere – perhaps at Nico's on the Zattere or Ruskin's favourite haunt at La Calcino.

Autumn

Season of mists. Some fog and days when the Vaporetto navigate by their radar. One day we were on a vaporetto near the Giardini stop in the early morning and the boat stopped and we were stunned to see an immense cruise liner emerge from out of the fog.

The film festival happens in September and you may catch a movie on the large screen in San Polo - these can sometimes link in with the Film Festival. It's a good time to visit the Biennale as the exhibitions continue into the Autumn.

The first high tides or Aqua Alta may happen. The duck boards appear ready for the streets being awash with water. The leaves are changing colour and vibrancy of autumn colours.

By November, however, the city is much quieter, the calles filled with locals and far fewer visitors. There can be bitter cold and sleet as winter takes hold of the city. Melancholy mists wrap Venice in a cloak of limited visibility and the vaporetto need to use their radar to navigate around the canals.

Mindful Walking in Autumn/Fall:

If you are in Venice in the Autumn then consider taking this walk (with boat ride) included.

This one is an adventure. Walk from where you are staying to Fondamenta Nova (if it is too far then take a vaporetto). Take the Number 12 vaporetto to Burano and get off at the Mazzorbo stop. Walk from Mazzorbo with its more rural aspect to the busier bustling Burano.

Wander through Burano to the Vaporetto station. Take a coffee somewhere near the boat stop and take in the scenery and locality flavour of this vibrant island village. The leaves may be turning colour or falling at this changing time of the year.

Take a different boat for the 5 minute journey to Torcello. Arrive at Torcello early in the morning and walk up the canal to the Basilica. You may be too early for it to be open – but today you are here for the walk. You should see seabirds and get a sense of the marshland environment. Pause at the Devil's Bridge and imagine when this was a built up and thriving city environment before falling into decay and disappearing back into the lagoon. It's almost like a Venetian Atlantis.

Make your way back to Burano and then to Venice by ferry or vaporetto. An early morning walk on the islands is an experience worth potentially missing breakfast for. Maybe pause on Burano on your return for a pastry (croissant) and coffee.

Autumn – Concerto in F Major

Allegro
The peasant celebrates with song and dance the harvest
safely gathered in.
The cup of Bacchus flows freely,
and many find their relief in deep slumber.

Adagio molto
The singing and the dancing die away
as cooling breezes fan the pleasant air,
inviting all to sleep
without a care.

Allegro
The hunters emerge at dawn,
ready for the chase,
with horns and dogs and cries.
Their quarry flees while they give chase.
Terrified and wounded, the prey struggles on,
but, harried, dies.

Winter

Of all the poems which inspired the Four Seasons Winter seems closest to reality in Venice. Listen to the music and the sound of icicles and frost in the music. My favourite movement is the Largo of winter.

Imagine the streets of Venice and the Largo music in your head - it fits so well as a soundtrack to the winter streets.

At some point the window boxes in the medieval buildings change from geraniums and begonias to cyclamen and violas or pansies. There are fewer frosts here because of the sea air but there is still a definite chill in the air. There can be whole days in November and December when the mist never lifts and the city is shrouded in a shift of fog and the buildings seem a different place. Then suddenly the sun may break through and it feels warm with the promise of warmer weather in the spring.

On average there is actually less rainfall in January than in other months. There can be lovely bright days in December. We've sat out in coats at Nicos on the Zattere in late December and sipped prosecco.

Winter months are punctuated by Christmas and then Carnivale.

Winter can be an eerie place of footsteps echoing along misty alleyways. It can be bitingly chilly when the Bora wind sweeps down from the Dolomites and damp air. But this is a quieter cityscape, with sudden days of blue sunny skies. Find a cafe, maybe Le Cafe in Santo Stefano or maybe stretch to Florians with its warm window seats for people watching in the wintry San Marco.

St Mark's Basilica is different in the wintertime. The basilica in winter is a shimmering, luminous golden place. The best time to visit is as dusk falls and the light fades and the golden light fills the interior. You may get the place almost to yourself.

It's nice to go in an air conditioned gallery or museum in the summer. But even more special when you have been walking in the biting cold and move into the warmth of the gallery. Visiting places like the Accademia and going in and out of the cold and then calling in a bar for a cappuccino or espresso and a pastry.

I've seen photos of Venice in the snow - I've never been there when it snowed but the muffling quality of the snow must give a magical experience - as long as you have boots with you of course. It's so hard to be mindful with cold feet.

Mindful Walking in Winter:

As Venice is quieter in the winter you could take this walk in the afternoon. The other walks are all early morning walks.

Set off at San Marco and walk all the way along the Riva degli Schiavoni. Pause at Via Garibaldi for a coffee. Either walk to the Giardino along the Riva and go in the Biennale entrance or walk along Via Garibaldi and enter the Giardini Gardens by that entrance.

Take a walk through the gardens. The Glass house Café is a good destination point for its quirky individuality and opportunity for a refreshing break.

Return via the Via Garibaldi and if you didn't go to the Glass house then take a coffee break at a bar here.

You can either return to San Marco by the Riva or past the Arsenale, through the streets of Castello, It's a lovely walk with many scenes of canals and calles and small campiellos.

If you were really tiring then sometimes it's 'just nice' to take a vaporetto from the Arsenale stop back to San Marco and float past the Riva and the Doges Palace.

Winter – Concerto in f-minor

Allegro non molto
Shivering, frozen mid the frosty snow in biting, stinging winds;
running to and fro to stamp one's icy feet,
teeth chattering in the bitter chill.

Largo
To rest contentedly beside the hearth,
while those outside are drenched by pouring rain.

Allegro
We tread the icy path slowly and cautiously,
for fear of tripping and falling.
Then turn abruptly, slip, crash on the ground and, rising,

hasten on across the ice lest it cracks up.
We feel the chill north winds coarse through the home
despite the locked and bolted doors...
this is winter,
which nonetheless brings its own delights.

251

Part 14

DEPARTING/FAREWELL

'One last look"

Venice, the most touristy place in the world, is still just completely magic to me

Frances Mayes

Taking & Making Memories

Sift through your memory bank and consider your best & most
beautiful memories ready to take home.

Days in Venice

Marble steps

Dark winter days

Christmas lights

Spring warmth

Bells and Wells

Lights on Grand Canal

Life on the Cannaregio Canal

Domes and Towers

Palazzos

Sheltered Islands

 Momento di Mindfulness
Curating a Collection of Views

During your days in Venice you are continually noticing views. This
may be wide panoramic vistas (and there are many of those). It may be
an interesting angel hiding on top of a church roof. Whatever the scenic
site you have been making a collection of views. Your mind has been
sifting and saving a collection of views for long term memory.

Scenes of La Serenissima
Close your eyes. Let the images of your favourite views float into your
thoughts.

Some will be wide vistas of the lagoon and the horizon. Some may be
narrow views of a calle. Maybe a window box with bright begonias. It

can be comforting sometimes to zoom in with a narrow focus shutting out wider clutter and noise.

Add any memories of sounds or music. Remember the temperature and whether it was a warm or chilly day. Was it still or breezy?

When you have completed this you know that when you close your eyes again you will see your favourite views. Now shuffle those views. Move the images slowly. Notice the details.

Make sure you 'view your views' several times over several hours so that the images become secured stored in your memory bank.

Reflect about returning home, where you are in life and how you want things to be when you return. You may want to live with more connection to the everyday moments, with less anxious thinking about life. Imagine yourself back at home and living your life in this way.

Almost time to leave your vacation or mindful mini break. Spending a few days being mindful in Venice may well have changed you. You should certainly have experiences and memories to take away when you leave.

Mindful thinking helps us to process the world around us in a more multi-sensory way. We begin to give attention and notice things like the breeze, the air temperature, the sunlight and shadows.

Keep doing this same visualising and shuffling of images. This process is going to help your return home and link any positive plans for change to your holiday memories. You now have a curated collection of images of your vacation and your life as you'd like it to be when you return home.

Whenever you do a mindful meditation at home then afterwards spend a few minutes viewing this 'mindful movie' of your vacation.

"Oh yes, it was my Venice! Beautiful,
With melancholy, ghostly beauty—old,
And sorrowful, and weary—yet so fair,
So like a queen still, with her royal robes,
Full of harmonious colour, rent and worn!"

Ada Cambridge,
The Manor House and Other Poems

Remembering Mindful Moments

Remember all your *Momento di Mindfulness*, those Mindful Moments in Venice and choose your favourite. Reflections on daily experience really do strengthen memories. Throughout '*Exploring Venice*' you've been working on developing your individual mental memory store. With the multi-sensory focus and by taking mindfulness 'out and about' with you on walks and boat rides you should have added strength and depth to your mindfulness practice.

Before you leave make sure you pack your Journal if you kept one. If you liked any of the poems or verse in 'Exploring Venice' then write out the words into your journal.

'One Last Look'

I always take 'one last look' wherever I visit. It's almost a transitional closure. I take a breath and focus on where I'm going next.

Remember if you have a long and tedious journey that you can reduce the reactive irritability of waiting in queues by utilising some of your learning in the Mindful Moments. Adjust your attitude to waiting, accept you have little influence over these things. Take an opportunity to breathe, observe and notice life around you.

One Last Look & Say Farewell for Now

Final Thoughts

"And if travel is like love, it is, in the end, mostly because it's a heightened state of awareness, in which we are mindful, receptive, in dimmed by familiarity and ready to be transformed. That is why the best trips, like the best love affairs, never really end."

Pico Iyer

Part 15

REFERENCES & RESOURCES

Accompanying Website

'Exploring Venice Mindfully'
has a linked Website

Here you will find photographs linked to the book.

www.mindfulvenice.com

Websites:

Body Scan Meditation:
UC San Diego Center for Mindfulness' 45 minute body scan meditation used in its trainings in Mindfulness-Based Stress Reduction available at https://www.mindful.org/

UCLA's Mindfulness Awareness Research Center (MARC) 3 minute body scan meditation available at https://www.mindful.org/

Mindfulness & Positive Psychology Related:
You Tube:
https://www.youtube.com/

Tara Brach:
https://www.tarabrach.com/

Lorin Roche and Camille Maurine
https://radiance-sutras.bandcamp.com/album/meditation-24-7

Mindful Website and Magazine
https://www.mindful.org/

Authentic Happiness:
https://www.authentichappiness.sas.upenn.edu/

Meditainment:
https://www.meditainment.com

Expressive Writing
https://www.psychologytoday.com/blog/write-yourself-well/201208/expressive-writing

Positive Psychology
https://positivepsychologyprogram.com/positive-psychology-exercises/

Venice & Travel Related Sites:

La Bussola Association
http://www.venicefreetours.com

The Wigwam Club (Gardens)
http://www.giardini-venezia.it/

La Toletta Bookshop & Centre
http://www.latoletta.com/

Rio Tera dei Pensieri Co-operative
https://www.rioteradeipensieri.org/en/

Art History by Dr Tom Nichols on Venetian Renaissance Art
(University of Glasgow)
https://www.thebritishacademy.ac.uk/blog/how-titian-paintings-rivalled-bellini

Matt Hershberger
https://matadornetwork.com/read/mindful-travel-going-next-big-thing/

Images of The Dolomites by Nicolo Miana
http://www.nicolomiana.com/dolomiti-da-venezia

https://www.smartertravel.com/mindful-travel-tips/

https://adventure.com/venice-overtourism-slow-travel/

https://www.smartertravel.com/mindful-travel-tips/

https://blog.insightvacations.com/secret-mindful-travel/

https://www.naturallyepicurean.org/single-post/2017/09/22/Abouteating-and-drinking-in-Venice-a-brief-guide-on-how-to-survive

Books:

Brach Tara 2013 True Refuge
Caldesi Katie & Caldesi Giancarlo 2014 Venice: Recipes Lost and Found
Clemence Sara 2017 Away & Aware: A Field Guide to Mindful Travel
Dammicco Mariagrazia, Majerus Marianne 2007 Venetian Gardens
Dammicco Mariagrazia Kostas Gabriele 2013 A guide to the gardens of Venice. Gardens, parks, orchards and fields in the city and on the islands
David Susan 2016 Emotional Agility
Dunant Sarah 2006 In the Company of the Courtesan
Gaffney Maureen 2011 Flourishing:
Germer Christopher K 2009 The Mindful Path to Self-Compassion
Gilbert Paul 2009 The Compassionate Mind: A new approach to life's challenges
Gonzalez Maria 2012 Mindful Leadership
Greenberg Melanie 2016 The Stress-proof Brain: Master Your Emotional Response to Stress Using Mindfulness and Neuroplasticity
Howes Ruth Riby 2018 Making Christmas Mindful
Iyer Pico 2014 The Art of Stillness: Adventures in Going Nowhere (TED)
Jonglez Thomas 2015 Secret Venice
Kabat-Zinn John 2016 (new edition) Wherever You Go, There You Are: Mindfulness meditation for everyday life
Kline Nancy 1999 Time to Think: Listening to Ignite the Human Mind
Leon Donna 2009 Death in a Strange County
Leon Donna 2009 Death at La Fenice
Leon Donna, Pianara Roberta 2010 A Taste of Venice: At Table with Brunetti
Lusk Julie 2017 Yoga Nidra for Complete Relaxation and Stress Relief
Marturano Janice 2014 Finding the Space to Lead: A Practical Guide to Mindful Leadership
Maurine Camille & Roche Lorin 2001 Meditation Secrets for Women
Melnick Sharon 2013 Success under Stress
Nichols Tom 2013 Titian and the End of the Venetian Renaissance
Neff Kristin 2015 Self Compassion: The proven Way of being Kind to Yourself
Norman Russell 2012 POLPO: A Venetian Cookbook (Of Sorts)
Patton Thoele Sue 2008 The Mindful Woman

Pennebaker James, Smyth Joshua 2016 Opening Up by Writing It Down, Third Edition: How Expressive Writing Improves Health and Eases Emotional

Richo David 2005 The Five Things we Cannot Change and the Happiness we find by Embracing them

Rowan Tiddy 2016 The Little Book of Mindful Travel

Seligman Martin 2009 Authentic Happiness: Using the new positive psychology to realise your potential for lasting fulfilment.

Seligman Martin 2011 Learned optimism: How to change your mind and your life

Sepeda Tony 2009 Brunetti's Venice: Walks Through the Novels

Sinclair Dr Michael 2013 Mindfulness for Busy People

Shamash Alidina 2015 The Mindful Way through Stress

Vickers Salley 2000 Miss Garnet's Angel

Webb Caroline 2016 How to have Good Day

Donna Leon's novels are easy to locate. Only two titles are given here.

APPENDIX

Opening Times
Always check opening times online or at Tourist Information. They can fluctuate in different seasons.

San Michele: Apr-Sep: 7.30am-6pm; rest of year: 7.30am-4.30pm (noon on 25 Dec and 1 Jan) @@@ opening times section.

San Giorgio:The Church stays open later than many of the Venetian churches. From April – October it is open daily from 9:00 until 19:00 hrs and from November – March from 8:30 until 18:00 hrs.

'Peggy's' opens late at 10:00 hrs and closes at 18:00 hrs. so it's a perfect visit for the end of a busy day.

The Redentore is open from 10.30- 16:30 hrs with last admission at 16:15 hrs.

The Salute is open from 15:00 – 17:50 hrs and often in the afternoon there is a musical Vespers while you wander quietly or sit and listen.

APPENDIX
Raisin Mindful Exercise

1. Holding: First, take a raisin and hold it in the palm of your hand or between your finger and thumb.

2. Seeing: Take time to really focus on it; gaze at the raisin with care and full attention—imagine that you've just dropped in from Mars and have never seen an object like this before in your life. Let your eyes explore every part of it, examining the highlights where the light shines, the darker hollows, the folds and ridges, and any asymmetries or unique features.

3. Touching: Turn the raisin over between your fingers, exploring its texture. Maybe do this with your eyes closed if that enhances your sense of touch.

4. Smelling: Hold the raisin beneath your nose. With each inhalation, take in any smell, aroma, or fragrance that may arise. As you do this, notice anything interesting that may be happening in your mouth or stomach.

5. Placing: Now slowly bring the raisin up to your lips, noticing how your hand and arm know exactly how and where to position it. Gently place the raisin in your mouth; without chY3ewing, noticing how it gets into your mouth in the first place. Spend a few moments focusing on the sensations of having it in your mouth, exploring it with your tongue.

6. Tasting: When you are ready, prepare to chew the raisin, noticing how and where it needs to be for chewing. Then, very consciously, take one or two bites into it and notice what happens in the aftermath, experiencing any waves of taste that emanate from it as you continue chewing. Without swallowing yet, notice the bare sensations of taste and texture in your mouth and how these may change over time, moment by moment. Also pay attention to any changes in the object itself.

7. Swallowing: When you feel ready to swallow the raisin, see if you can first detect the intention to swallow as it comes up, so that even this is experienced consciously before you actually swallow the raisin.

8. Following: Finally, see if you can feel what is left of the raisin moving down into your stomach, and sense how your body as a whole is feeling after you have completed this exerci

About The Author

Ruth Riby Howes lives in North Yorkshire with her husband and a medium-sized cross breed dog (part Jack Russell and who knows what else!) called Pliny. Originally from the seaside town of Scarborough (you can hear the sea from her parents' house) she is now living in the Yorkshire Dales.

Ruth works full time in the NHS and writing is a part time interest. A professional 'day job' interest in positive therapy, communication skills and mindful leadership guides her writing. The work of Penn State University in Positive Psychology has been inspirational as it focuses on what maintains wellbeing and enables people to feel "as happy as they can be".

The 'Approaching Christmas Mindfully' Series began in 2017 and in 2018 was combined into the single volume 'Making Christmas Mindful'. This is a guide to pausing, noticing, reflecting on life and relationships and by utilising some of the varied mindful and positive therapy strategies making that 'Happy Christmas' more likely.

This book 'Exploring Venice Mindfully' is a new departure. A guide for sight seeking in combination with suggestions for mindful exploration of the city. The regular 'Mindful Moments' are designed to strengthen mindfulness during a vacation.

Ruth has visited Venice regularly since she was a child and this book gives her the opportunity to shares her knowledge and experience as a visitor to La Serenissima.

Made in the USA
Las Vegas, NV
03 September 2021